Child Of God

Entering the Fullness of Your Inheritance in Christ

Child Of God

Entering the Fullness of Your Inheritance in Christ

E. C. Nakeli

King's Word Publishing

© 2016 by E.C. Nakeli

Published by King's Word Publication

For your questions and publishing needs, write to:

> CMFI
> 40 S Church st
> Westminster, MD 21157
> E-mail: ecnakeli@yahoo.com

Printed in the United States of America

All rights reserved. No part of this publication may be reproduced, stored in a retrieval systems, or transmitted in ay form or by any means— for example, electronic, photocopy, recording—without the prior written permission of the publisher. The only exception is brief quotations in printed reviews.

E.C. Nakeli

To contact the author, write to:

> E.C. Nakeli
> 40 S Church st
> Westminster, MD 21157
> E-mail: ecnakeli@yahoo.com

Child of God/ E.C. Nakeli

ISBN: 978-1-945055-00-3

> Unless otherwise indicated, Scriptures references are from
> THE HOLY BIBLE, NEW INTERNATIONAL VERSION®, NIV®
> Copyright © 1973, 1978, 1984, 2011 by Biblica, Inc™
> Used by permission. All rights reserved worlwide.

Cover and Interior Design: Zach Essama

Table of Contents

Chapter 1: God's Creation 1
Chapter 2: Two Kingdoms 5
Chaper 3: Identifying Yourself 19
Chapter 4: Child of God 29
Chapter 5: The Grace of the Child 35
Chapter 6: The Hope of a Child 41
Chaper 7: The Child's Freedom 49
Chapter 8: The Child's Victory 59
Chapter 9: The Child's Health 69
Chapter 10: The Child's Privileges 73
Chapter 11: The Child's Privileges 2 83
Chapter 12: The Child's Privileges 3 93
Chapter 13: The Child's Privileges 4 99
Chapter 14: The Child's Responsibility 107
Chapter 15: The Child's Responsibility 2 113
Chapter 16: The Child's Responsibility 3 127
Chapter 17: More than just a Child 135
Chapter 18: The Child as a Friend 145
Chapter 19: The Child as a Slave 153
Chapter 20: The Child in the Father's Army 159
Chapter 21: The Child as Lighh 169
Conclusion 173

Chapter 1

God's Creation

"In the beginning God created the heavens and the earth" (Genesis 1:1).

In the beginning God created the universe and all that is in it; the heavens and all that is in them; the stars, the moon, the planets, the sun, the sky, the ozone layer, the galaxies-billions of them, the milky way, the earth and all that is in it; from the animals, to plants and humans. More than that, God created things visible and invisible.

> *"The earth is the LORD's, and everything in it, the world, and all who live in it; for he founded it upon the seas and established it upon the waters"* (Psalm 24:1-2).

By right of creation, God owns everything in the world, from the most microscopic organism to the most gigantic. From the most primitive animal to the most developed mankind. God owns you and me because He owns *"the world, and all who live in it"* and because *"He founded it upon the seas and established it upon the waters."* Yes all things were created by God – the great Jehovah, Three in one.

> *"For by him all things were created: things in heaven and on earth, visible and invisible, whether thrones or powers or rulers or authorities; all things were created by him and for him" (Colossians 1:16).*

The powers of darkness in rebellion against Him, mankind in rebellion against Him, creation in rebellion against Him, Angels in loyalty to Him, His church in loyalty to Him were all created for Him and by Him. Nothing exists which He did not make. (John 1:3). Some were made as "object of his wrath", others as object of his infinite Love. So from the word, we have seen that God made everything. Satan created nothing, and he can create nothing. What he has done and still does is to cause God's creation to rebel against the Creator God – Jehovah Elohim. He may use things to accomplish his selfish end but he did not make any of them. He seeks ever to pervert nature and the order of things. Of course he can only use things which are in rebellion against the Creator God.

The Old Order

If you read the account of creation in Genesis chapters one and two, you'll realise that among all things created, man was very last and God made him on the last day of creation. Everything was "prepared" for man to come and possess. It is like a child born into a family where everything has already been acquired for him and all he needs do is to manage the estate he inherits. Man had no limitation whatsoever to his rule over things on the earth. As long as the earth was concerned, man's dominion was to know no bound whatsoever on land, in the sea and in the air: the animals, the fishes and the birds.

Thus I have said that in the old order, man was created last, not because he was least, but because God wanted all that man needed to be available and may be for other reasons not revealed in scripture. Man was to be the most responsible of all creation. Man was the only thing given the privilege to be made in God's own image. God said "let there be" and "it was so" for everything that exists but for man He said "let us make". It was a matter of making; time invested, wisdom, care, expertise etc. combined by Father, Son, and Holy Spirit.

Unfortunately, something went wrong, and may be an emergency meeting was called in heaven to address the situation: it was the crises of the fall, which led to the curse. The whole of heaven was mobilised; man had been deceived and led into rebellion by Satan the devil; the whole of man's dominion changed ownership into the hands of the rebel of all times. Man proved the most irresponsible. It is like a Father who gives his son a vast part of his estate to manage, only to come one day and realize that in defiance of a simple warning given to him, everything has been transferred to the ownership of another – his arch enemy. The son, instead of coming to report the incident to the father, runs way and hides from his father. Man did just that and in the twinkling of an eye lost everything that was given him.

The New Order

In the new order, after the fall and after all creation rebelled, God decided to bring all things back under His rule. In this mission of recreation, God has decided that all things will be made new. He is going to recreate the universe and all things must be destroyed, for new ones to be made. In this new order, man has been given the privilege to be the first to be reconciled to God, through Christ's dead on the cross of Calvary.

> "...and through him to reconcile to himself all things, whether things on earth or things in heaven, by making peace through his blood, shed on the cross" (Colossians 1:20).

The purpose of Christ's dead on the cross is that through Him all visible and invisible things on earth and in heaven should be reconciled to God. This includes animals, plants, nature and everything that was led into the rebellion, except Satan and his demons, doomed for destruction. Through this reconciliation, God restores to man the dignity, dominion and authority which he forfeited through disobedience. Until the second coming of Jesus, the rest of creation will not experience this recreation process. It is then that everything will be made new. There shall be a new heaven and a new earth.

> *"Behold, I will create new heavens and a new earth. The former things will not be remembered, nor will they come to mind" (Isaiah 65:17) (See also Revelations 21:1).*

The old heavens and earth will all be destroyed when Jesus Christ shall come

> *"But the day of the Lord will come like a thief. The heavens will disappear with a roar; the elements will be destroyed by fire, and the earth and everything in it will be laid bare" (2 Peter 3:10).*

Until this day, the rest of creation has to wait, and it does so in "eager expectation". As in the beginning where the heavens and the earth were created first and completed, so man has been given this same opportunity to be recreated first in this new order. Man's "day of recreation" will soon be over and that will be all. God will then move over to recreating the new heaven and the new earth. Thus, until Jesus comes, everyman is given the opportunity to be recreated. After that it will be all over, no more recreation for man. It shall be the "day of recreation" for the rest of nature.

Chapter 2

Two Kingdoms

God created the whole universe to be under His control. It was His original purpose that all creation will submit to His loving rule. He purposed everything to be under one kingdom – the kingdom of God. For billions of years, there was just one kingdom – God's own kingdom - until Satan in pride decided and said to himself *"I will make myself like the Most High"*. He sought to establish his own kingdom, but since he wasn't the creator, he could create nothing. In his scheme he seduced a third of the angels in heaven to rebel against God and question His sovereignty and rule. The Bible says of Satan,

> *"'You were the model of perfection, full of wisdom and perfect in beauty. You were in Eden, the garden of God; every precious stone adorned you: ruby, topaz and emerald, chrysolite, onyx and jasper, sapphire, turquoise and beryl. Your settings and mountings were made of gold; on the day you were created they were prepared. You were anointed as a guardian cherub, for so I ordained you. You were on the holy mount of God; you walked among the fiery stones. You were blameless in your ways from the day you were created till wickedness was found in you. Through your widespread trade you were filled with violence, and you sinned. So I drove you in disgrace from the mount of God, and I expelled you, O guardian cherub, from among the fiery stones. Your heart became proud on account of your beauty, and you corrupted your wisdom*

> because of your splendor. So I threw you to the earth; I made a spectacle of you before kings. By your many sins and dishonest trade you have desecrated your sanctuaries. So I made a fire come out from you, and it consumed you, and I reduced you to ashes on the ground in the sight of all who were watching" (Ezekiel 28:12^b-18).

When was wickedness found in him? The day he said in his heart:

> "I will ascend to heaven; I will raise my throne above the stars of God; I will sit enthroned on the mount of assembly, on the utmost heights of the sacred mountain. I will ascend above the tops of the clouds; I will make myself like the Most High" (Isaiah 14:13-14).

It was his purpose to establish his own kingdom, where all praise and honor will come to him, so he decided to raise his "throne above the stars of God", he sought a kingdom in which even the Most High, would be subject to him, his purpose was to overthrow the throne of God and establish his, but unfortunately for him he was thrown to the earth and made a spectacle by Michael and his angels. Satan and his group of rebellious angels had no place to exercise their rule. He had nothing he could use to build a kingdom for himself, so man became his target. When he succeeded to deceive man, ownership of man's dominion was transferred to Satan and man himself became subject to this enemy of his soul.

The Bible says Satan was the *"model of perfection, full of wisdom and perfect in beauty."* He used this wisdom and perfect beauty to establish his kingdom, carefully planned and organized in rebellion against God. This is what the Bible refers to as the world. Jesus Christ distinguished His Kingdom from that of the world (John 18:36) and called Satan the *"god of this world"*.

The Kingdom of Satan

This includes the world (what it is).

This system has its

1. Ways .... Ephesians 2:2 (course NKJV)
2. Wisdom .... 1 Corinthians 3:19
3. Passions .... Titus 2:12
4. Cares .... Matthew 13:22, Mark 14:19 (NKJV)
5. Ruler .... John 14:30 (NKJV)
6. Spirit .... 1 Corinthians 2:12 (Ephesians 2:2)
7. Principles .... Galatians 4:3, Col 2:8
8. Men .... Psalm 17:14
9. Weapons .... 1 Corinthians 10:4
10. Worldly Sorrow .... 2 Corinthians 7:9

The Ruler of the World

> *"I will no longer talk much with you, for the ruler of this world is coming, and he has nothing in Me"* (John 14:30, NKJV).

We already said Satan is the ruler of this world, a system organized in rebellion against God. This system is organized both in the visible and in the invisible realms, the visible controlled by the invisible.

In the invisible, the system is organized into what the Bible calls the rulers, authorities, powers and spiritual forces of evil (Ephesians 6:12 NIV). The NKJV version puts it better:

1. Principalities
2. Powers
3. Rulers
4. Hosts of wickedness

Each level has its representative in the council of hell, where new philosophies and methods of sin are invented. The president of this council is Satan himself. He presides over every meeting to ensure that there is no rebellion, for he trusts none of his subjects. Satan has under him hundreds of thousands or even millions of principalities. These in turn have under them powers in their numbers. The powers have as subjects, rulers to execute their orders. These rulers have millions of hosts of wickedness who enforce all that is determined in the council of hell. They are the ones who came in contact with human beings – bound to them through covenants they probably entered into knowingly or unknowingly. These are the ones who through the mind seek to impose their ways, principles, and attitudes in the heart of man.

The Bible also refers to this organized system as the dominion of darkness. It is a whole structure put in place to enforce Satan's rule and to lure man as far away from God as possible. It is put in place to keep man's view of the Creator as blurred as possible. The principalities inspire false religions and doctrines, so that man is kept from finding Jesus Christ – the Way. Satan is called *"the ruler of the kingdom of the air"* (Ephesians 2:2).

The Spirit of this world

> *"…in which you used to live when you followed the ways of this world and of the ruler of the kingdom of the air,* ***the spirit who is now at work*** *in those who are disobedient"* (Ephesians 2:2, emphasis mine).

Just as God gives his children the Holy Spirit who is God's own Spirit, to lead them into good works and all that God has in store for them, Satan has his spirit called the spirit of this world (1Corinthians 2:12). This spirit is at work in the children of the kingdom of the world, the children of Satan. It seeks to promote all forms of godlessness. It seeks to propagate the ways, principles, values, cares etc. of this world, in order to keep men bound to Satan.

The ways or course of this world

> "…*in which you used to live when you followed* **the ways of this world** *and of the ruler of the kingdom of the air, the spirit who is now at work in those who are disobedient*" (Ephesians 2:2, emphasis mine).

This world has ways: ways of doing things, ways of planning etc.

All this ways are arranged perfectly in a course which the NKJV calls the course of this world. All that happens in the world today is due to the course-the stream in which things move. This course is nothing but rebellion, for that is the main driving motive of its ruler. The psalmist terms this: *"the way of sinners"* (Psalm 1:1) In other words it is the way of sin, the way of the wicked (Proverbs 4:19) which the Bible invites him to forsake (Isaiah 55: 7).

This is a way of viewing people and things from a selfish point of view; what you can obtain from them and not what you can give. It is the way which says you should always be on the advantage; always defend your rights etc.

Remember we said these are ways of a course- the course of this world, which is rebellion against God and all that is called authority with the end as destruction. God has promised to destroy the world and its system, and so all who are part of it will end up in the lake of fire.

The passion of this world

> "*It teaches us to say "No" to ungodliness and worldly passions, and to live self-controlled, upright and godly lives in this present age*" (Titus 2:12).

The world today is characterised by the desire for pleasure, gain, wealth, honor and power. A mad craze for power! People will do everything to obtain power, from cheating to bloodshed. The quest for gain and wealth has always been on the rise and men will hold nothing back to obtain it, even to the point of forfeiting their souls. There is a passion for pleasure that leads to sensual lust, increased desire for illicit sex, drugs, orgies and all that leads to debauchery.

This is what the Bible refers to as the desire of the flesh or sinful desire. The world thinks that responding fully to these desires will satisfy them completely. That is why sensual lusts and indulgence is on the rise. Each new day, a new breed of perverts surfaces on the horizon. More and more, dresses are made to expose the sexual parts of the body, music is made in order to arouse sensual passion and more people get entangled and bound to the destruction of their souls. This is what the Bible terms; Passionate lust (Thessalonians 4:5), or the lust of the eyes (1 John 2:16).

The Principles or Philosophies of the World

> *"So also, when we were children, we were in slavery under the basic principles of the world"* (Galatians 4:3).

> *"See to it that no one takes you captive through hollow and deceptive philosophy, which depends on human tradition and the basic principles of this world rather than on Christ"* (Colossians 2:8).

The principles of the world are quite different from those of God's kingdom. The former is a principle of hating your enemies and cursing those who curse you. It is that of fighting back when you feel cheated, doing good to those who are good to you, and lending were you will make the greatest profit. It is the principle of *"life for life, eye for eye, tooth for tooth, hand for hand, foot for foot, burn for burn, wound for wound, and bruise for bruise."* These are philosophies which seek to put man at the centre of everything; man is regarded as supreme and accountable to no one for his actions and decisions. It is a system whose aim is to promote man's *"independence"* from God. It puts forth man as the solution to his own problems. These philosophies are

1. hollow
2. deceptive
3. depend on human tradition
4. depend on basic worldly principles

- They are hollow because though outwardly they appear to offer something; inside they are just empty, with nothing to offer. They seem to have substance but inwardly there is a vacuum and a void.
- They are deceptive because they don't lead where they pretend to lead to. They seem to offer joy but in the end it is sorrow; happiness but in the end pains. In reality these philosophies hide their "truth" from those who believe in them. They offer glory but bring only shame. For each thing offered, 95% has some hidden flaw or danger which many innocently reap.
- They depend on human tradition and this tradition changes from generation to generation. They tell you one thing today, and tomorrow it is something else. Today it is this mode and tomorrow another. The traditions of men have no other goal but to lure your soul away from the principles of God's kingdom. Those who follow it will like the Pharisees, totally keep aside the laws of God.
- The worldly philosophy depends on worldly principles which have no goal but to keep the soul of man in slavery to the old man.

The wisdom of this world (Fleshly wisdom)

"For the wisdom of this world is foolishness in God's sight. As it is written: 'He catches the wise in their craftiness'" (1 Corinthians 3:19).

"Now this is our boast: Our conscience testifies that we have conducted ourselves in the world, and especially in our relations with you, in the holiness and sincerity that are from God. We have done so not according to worldly wisdom but according to God's grace" (2 Corinthians 1:2).

The wisdom of the world is aimed at bringing God to the sphere of human thinking. It originates in carnal man as he seeks solution to his problems independently of God. Worldly wisdom says *"How can this be done without the intervention of God? How can this be done independently of God?"* It tries to bring everything to reason. God's ways and principles are brought to questioning, directly or indirectly. The Bible says *"God has made foolish the wisdom of this world"*. No matter how high the world esteems its wisdom, it remains *"foolishness in God's sight"*. Worldly wisdom questions and doubts God's grace and seeks in every plane to associate works of merit to God's love package - salvation. The Bible says worldly or earthly wisdom is unspiritual and of the devil. Satan is the origin of the wisdom of this world.

The Cares and Worries of this World

> *Now he who received seed among the thorns is he who hears the word, and the cares of this world and the deceitfulness of riches choke the word, and he becomes unfruitful"* (Matthew 13:22, NKJV).

The Bible also talks of the cares of this world which prevent the healthy growth of God's word in the heart of man. They prevent the word from bearing any mature fruit in the heart of the individual who harbors them. I find no other passage in the Bible which better describe these cares than Matthew 6:25-34

> *"Therefore I tell you, do not worry about your life, what you will eat or drink; or about your body, what you will wear. Is not life more important than food, and the body more important than clothes? Look at the birds of the air; they do not sow or reap or store away in barns, and yet your heavenly Father feeds them. Are you not much more valuable than they? Who of you by worrying can add a single hour to his life? And why do you worry about clothes? See how the lilies of the field grow. They do not labor or spin. Yet I tell you that not even Solomon in his entire splendor was dressed like one of these. If that is how God clothes the grass of the field, which is here today and tomorrow is thrown into the fire, will he not much more clothe you, O you of little faith? So do not worry, saying, 'What shall we eat?' or 'What shall we drink?' or 'What shall we wear?' For the pagans run after all these things, and your heavenly Father knows that you need them"* (Matthew 6:25-34).

People of this world know nothing but the cares of life, how one can eat well, what one can eat and drink etc. They plan today what shall be eaten next week. All their efforts are tied to this life. They care about what they wear and work tirelessly for it. For many have become slaves to their stomach and to their body to a point where health and even life is sacrificed so the body and stomach could be worshipped. Their days are full of questions of *"what shall we eat?" "What shall we drink?" "What shall we wear?" "What does the future hold?" "What about this or that business?"* All they know is anxiety in one form or another.

All that does not involve seeking God's kingdom is a worldly care. All that will not help you or any man to move closer to God but instead draw you away from all that concerns God and His kingdom is a worldly care, no matter how genuine it may appear. It may be the quest for a better car, a better home or just things that lead to ease, comfort and pleasure.

Wordly Sorrow

"Godly sorrow brings repentance that leads to salvation and leaves no regret, but worldly sorrow brings death" (2 Corinthians 7:10).

This is sorrow that mostly results from failure to accomplish selfish ends and ambitions. It leads to self-condemnation, hopelessness and emptiness. It leads to revenge, hatred and its sister vices. Many suicides in the world today, if not all, can be traced to worldly sorrow which led to despair and a sense of feeling useless. The end of worldly sorrow is death be it to the individual or the object of his vengeance.

Should we talk of the weapons, the values, the standards and things of this world? The list can go on and on. However, we shall not end this discussion without talking about the children of this world.

The Children of this World

"Jesus said to them, 'if God was your Father, you would love me, for I came from God and now am here. I have not come on my own; but he sent me. Why is my language not clear to you? Because you are unable to hear what I say. You belong to your father, the devil, and you want to carry out your father's desire. He was a murderer from the beginning, not holding to the truth, for there is no truth in him. When he lies, he speaks his native language, for he is a liar and the father of lies. Yet because I tell the truth, you do

> *not believe me! Can any of you prove me guilty of sin? If I am telling the truth, why don't you believe me? He who belongs to God hears what God says. The reason you do not hear is that you do not belong to God.'"* (John 8:42-46).

This passage describes those who live according to the ways, principles, influence, values and standards of the world. They follow the course of this world and are rebellious to God. They hate God and have refused to have anything to do with His salvation. The language of the gospel of Jesus Christ is never clear to them. They practice sin in one form or another, and carryout the desires of Satan the devil: lies, murder, idolatry, sexual immorality, just to name a few.

They are those the Bible refers to as children of wrath (Ephesians 2:2,3), for at the end what awaits them is God's wrath. They are sons of disobedience, those who give themselves to the lusts of the flesh, live in fulfillment of the desires of the flesh and mind and are dead in their trespasses. Yes dead in their trespasses as they are insensitive to the life of God and all it offers. Their consciences are dead with respect to anything which has to do with God, His kingdom, righteousness and holiness. Their only interest is in this life. Their labor, toil, projects and investments are only in this life. They fail to have a view of eternity. The Psalmist said,

> *"O LORD, by your hand save me from such men, from men of this world whose reward is in this life"* (Psalm 17:14a).

Men and women whose rewards are only in this life are children of this world. The other life holds nothing for them but endless woe and agony. In this we also find the category which claims to know God but deny His truth and His ways. They seem to be *"having a form of godliness but denying its power"*.

They are *"lovers of themselves, lovers of money, boastful, proud, abusive, disobedient to their parents, ungrateful, unholy, without love, unforgiving, slanderous, without self-control, brutal, not lovers of the good, treacherous, rash, and conceited, lovers of pleasure rather than lovers of God-- having a form of godliness but denying its power"* (2Timothy 3:2-5).

By nature and choice, such people have pledged allegiance consciously or unconsciously to Satan and are living under the influence of the satanic trinity —the Devil, the flesh and the world.

Having said much about the kingdom of Satan, which is a counterfeit kingdom, let's talk about the kingdom of God, the one and only legitimate kingdom.

The Kingdom of God

This kingdom is before the beginning of time, it is the one legitimate kingdom which exists in the universe. Until the rebellion it had been the only kingdom, the kingdom of peace, of love, of holiness; the kingdom of faith, hope and righteousness. The kingdom of God has supremacy over Satan's kingdom just as God is infinitely superior to Satan. The kingdom is and is to come in all fullness of glory and splendor. It stands for all time and for eternity. This kingdom is also called the kingdom of heaven and justice is her scepter. It equally has ways, principles and values, a Ruler, a Spirit, a course, wisdom and much more.

The Ruler of the Kingdom of God

The ruler of the Kingdom of God is no one else but the Eternal Son of God, Jesus Christ. He not only rules the kingdom of God but rules the whole wide universe. Everything in heaven and on earth obeys His word. He is the eternal King of ages. *"The ruler of God's creation…"* (Revelation 3:14). The Bible says *"He is before all things"* (Colossians 1:17) *"and God placed all things under his feet and appointed him to be head over everything"* (Ephesians 1:22). After His resurrection He said, *"All authority in heaven and on earth has been given to me"* (Matthew 20:18).

The Spirit of the Kingdom of God

The Spirit of the kingdom of God is God's own Spirit, the Holy Spirit. He is the third Person of the Holy Trinity. He has been at work since from before the foundations of the universe.

The Bible Says,

> *"Now the earth was formless and empty, darkness was over the surface of the deep, and the Spirit of God was hovering over the waters"* (Genesis 1:2).

Throughout Bible history, He has manifested Himself in diverse ways, leading God's people, teaching God's people etc. He is currently the Director of kingdom activities here on planet earth. There's much that can be said about Him. We shall treat this in a book *"The Person and Ministry of the Holy Spirit."* For now, suffice it to say that He is the Spirit of God's Kingdom, working in the lives of God's elect, advancing God's kingdom and the formation of Christ in all those who name His Name.

The Ways of the Kingdom

The ways of the kingdom of God are God's own ways; they originate in the person of God, and are promoted by God. Everyone in God's kingdom has been called to walk in those ways. His ways are different and higher than the ways of men.

> *"'For my thoughts are not your thoughts, neither are your ways my ways', declares the LORD. As the heavens are higher than the earth, so are my ways higher than your ways and my thoughts than your thoughts"* (Isaiah 55:8-9).

The Bible reveals the ways of God in a detailed manner; the way of justice, the way of holiness, truth etc. The ways of God are tied to obedience. Those who walk in His ways view people in terms of what they can offer them. Those who walk according to these ways offer themselves to be used by the heavenly Father to reach out to those in need, those in pain, the hopeless, the suffering and above all the lost. The ways of the kingdom are tied to a course. This course is led by Jesus Christ to swing the world back to its first allegiance and bring everything to subjection and obedience to God. The course is to destroy all rebellion from the face of the earth and project God's supremacy. Every child of God is called to seek these ways, through prayer and their diligent study of the scriptures.

The Principles of the Kingdom

The kingdom of God has principles under which it operates. These principles were established by God at the very foundation of the world. They remain unchanging from age to age. They are revealed in what the Bible terms in Psalm 119:

- The Laws of God .... Vs 1
- The precepts of God .... Vs 4
- The statutes of God .... Vs 2
- The decrees of God .... Vs 5
- The commands of God .... Vs 6

Actually, there is not much difference between the ways and the principles of the Kingdom. When someone is filled with desire for the Kingdom, automatically, he begins to direct his life according to the ways and principles of God. To him who seeks them, they become a delight, a guide, counsel, a source of strength, a source of hope and life. Above all, the principles that govern this Kingdom are based on the supreme principle of love which leads to forgiveness.

The Values of the Kingdom

In God's kingdom everything is valued with respect to its impact in the Kingdom. Everything is viewed in the perspective of how it pleases the heart of God, how it glorifies God, how it helps in expansion and advancement of God's Kingdom. Everything is evaluated based on how it can take one closer to God in love, intimacy, holiness, knowledge and service; how it can help one in the formation of Christ in one's life. In other words, in this Kingdom, things are evaluated with respect to their eternal values, that is, how they help us to better prepare for eternity and be ready for Christ's return. It is on this basis that decisions, choices, and priorities are made.

Chapter 3

Identifying Yourself

Remember we said that, there are only two kingdoms in the universe today; one a breakaway kingdom and the other, the legitimate kingdom. Each of us belongs to one of these kingdoms as proven by the daily choices we make, the ways we follow, the course we are advocating, the principles we live by, the things we value and the ruler we obey. But there is something more to that. By nature, all human beings are born children of the devil. That's why the Bible says we were by nature children of wrath. All of us at one time before ever being saved (those who are) belonged here. We lived in obedience to the satanic trinity – the devil, the flesh, the world.

The children of God and the children of Satan are identified not just by what they profess but by how they live: *"This is how we know who the children of God are and who the children of the devil are: Anyone who does not do what is right is not a child of God; nor is anyone who does not love his brother."* (1John 3:10). To be more explicit, *"He who does what is sinful is of the devil, because the devil has been sinning from the beginning. The reason the Son of God appeared was to destroy the devil's work"* (1 John 3:8).

In your daily life, what are the things which motivate and characterize your actions? What are your values in life? On what bases do you make your choices? To what do you give most of your time, especially your spare time? Only an honest answer to the above questions, in the light of what has been shared can let you know truly where you belong. There're many, who are so deceived and swept away by presumption that they never care to face these realities. They magnify God's love and mercy and use it as a license to godlessness yet forget that God is a God of justice, of truth, and of holiness, and that *"He will judge the world in righteousness and the peoples in His truth"* (Psalm 96:13b).

It is for this reason that the apostle Paul wrote to the church of the Corinthians:

> *"Do you not know that the wicked will not inherit the kingdom of God? Do not be deceived: Neither the sexually immoral nor idolaters nor adulterers nor male prostitutes nor homosexual offenders nor thieves nor the greedy nor drunkards nor slanderers nor swindlers will inherit the kingdom of God"* (1 Corinthians 6:9-10).

Yet there're many, so deceived, who've never known the saving power of Jesus Christ from their sins. Year by year they live in Christian circles but would rather die than to separate themselves from the sin they so cherish. To such, I say things are even worse, far worse than for the heathen because it is written that,

> *"If we deliberately keep on sinning after we have received the knowledge of the truth, no sacrifice for sins is left, but only a fearful expectation of judgment and of raging fire that will consume the enemies of God. Anyone who rejected the Law of Moses died without mercy on the testimony of two or three witnesses. How much more severely do you think a man deserves to be punished who has trampled the Son of God under foot, who has treated as an unholy thing the blood of the covenant that sanctified him, and who has insulted the Spirit of grace? For we know him who said, "It is mine to avenge; I will repay," and again, "The Lord will judge his people." It is a dreadful thing to fall into the hands of the living God"* (Hebrews 10:26-31).

Let me ask you a question, do you claim to know the truth and yet continue in your sin? This is a most wicked thing a man can ever do. Let me point out three very awful things you do to the Godhead.

1. You trample the Son of God underfoot.
2. You treat as an unholy thing the blood of the covenant that sanctified you.
3. You insult the Spirit of grace (Hebrews 10:29).

In the words of the writer of Hebrew, for you *"nothing is left but a fearful expectation of judgment and of fire that will consume the enemies of God"*.

God terms you His enemy, how can you then belong to His kingdom? May be you are Satan's man in *"God's side"*.

May be in all honesty, you have realized you're not God's child, we shall see how to become one. Remember there's no neutral ground and no one belongs to both: your values, choices and priorities in life determine where you belong. Maybe before we talk on how to become a child, since we've talked much about who's not a child of God, let's talk a bit about who is a child, so you can better evaluate your stance, and face things squarely.

Who's a Child of God

"Even a child is known by his actions, by whether his conduct is pure and right" (Proverbs 20:11).

This applies to children of God. They're known by their actions, whether their conducts are pure and right. These are those who pursue righteousness and purity in all they do. God's holiness is what determines their day to day action. They live by what is right and pure, walk by what is right and pure, and conduct themselves in purity and righteousness whether in private or public - in the most secluded of places or the most crowded. Their actions, choices, priorities are not determined by time or space. Put them in the most primitive village or in the most civilized city, their actions and conduct will be the same, for they always seek to live and model their lives in the light of God's unchanging word because, *"He who belongs to God hears what God says"* (John 8:47a).

Here, to hear means to listen or pay attention to something or to somebody. What is your attitude towards God's word, His word written in the Bible, His word spoken to you through His messengers, His word spoken to you in the private? Do you pay attention to God's word? Do you heed His invitation and the warnings found in the Bible?

Jesus made it categorically clear that children of God pay attention to what God says, their consciences are alive towards the word of God, they respond to the things of God.

Becoming a Child

Most of what we'll treat here could have been mentioned in the last section. But so we can better understand how to become and remain a child of God, I've decided to treat it under this section.

How to be Saved

> *"But we ought always to thank God for you, brothers loved by the Lord, because from the beginning God chose you to be saved through the sanctifying work of the Spirit and through belief in the truth"* (2 Thessalonians 2:13).

Here, we see two things that work out salvation:-

1. Belief in the truth
2. The sanctifying work of the Holy Spirit.

1. Belief in the Truth

The question one may ask, like Pilate did, is *"what is truth?"* Truth is that Jesus Christ is the Son of God, that He is God the Son, the Way the Truth and the Life, the one and only Mediator between God and man. The truth is that there's an enemy – Satan, that there's a hell, that we cannot save ourselves, that apart from Christ, all our deeds of righteousness are like filthy rags before God, that all have sinned and fallen short of God's glory, and that Jesus came to save sinners and restore us back to God. That is the truth; they are not truths but the truth. They are inseparable, you can't believe one and leave out the other, all are in God's word, and God's word is truth; and unless you believe all of it, then you can as well forget it. The next point I want to draw is that, there's more than just believing in the truth, James says *"even the demons believe that and shudder"* (James 2:19).

What you have believed is now acted out. How? By deciding to turn away from all sin, and inviting Jesus into your life, for him to give you the power to live above sin.

> *"Yet to all who received him, to those who believed in his name, he gave the right to become children of God"* (John 1:12).

If you invite Jesus Christ into your life, He'll give you the right to become a child of God, a child, *"born not of natural descent, nor of human decision or a husband's will, but born of God"*. Another version puts it that *"He gave them power to become children of God"*.

A godly life can only be led by those to whom this power has been given. On our own, we can't live as God's children; we do not have the power to overcome the temptations which always surround us, this power can only come from the Son of God. This is the power you need to break loose from the sinful habits you're so accustomed to. And until you've received Jesus, until you've believed in His Name, this power can never be your portion.

Do you believe in His Name: the saving power of His Name, the holiness of His Name, the authority of His Name, and the might of His Name? So, *"you also were included in Christ when you heard the word of truth, the gospel of your salvation. Having believed, you were marked in him with a seal, the promised Holy Spirit, who is a deposit guaranteeing our inheritance until the redemption of those who are God's possession—to the praise of his glory"* (Ephesians 1:13,14).

The Holy Spirit is the only guarantee we have as children of God. He is the One *"guaranteeing our inheritance"* and He *"testifies with our spirit that we are God's children"* (Romans 8:16).

Is there a testimony to your spirit by the Spirit of truth that *"you are a child of God"*? Then rest assured for *"if our hearts do not condemn us, we have confidence before God"* (I John 3:7).

Continuing as a Child

2. The Sanctifying Work of the Holy Spirit

This is a process which begins at conversion and ends when the child goes to meet the Father, yet it is an integral part of our salvation. The Holy Spirit's task in each life is to conform it to the person of Jesus Christ. That's why He has to lead us, and as we follow, we will all be brought into His likeness. Is this not why the Bible categorically states that, *"those who are led by the Spirit of God are sons of God"* (Romans 8:14)?

You see, it does not end at believing in His Name, though that's the very foundation of it all, it goes beyond that to the level of being *"led by the Spirit of God"* in our daily choices. It is He who leads us, directs and molds us into the objects and people God wants us to be. Only those who obey Him, respond to His leadership and are sensitive to His promptings can have Him do His work of sanctification in their lives.

Shall we not stop for a moment, with brokenness of heart and contrition of spirit, and ask God to forgive us for our strong wills, our hardened hearts etc. which make the work of the Spirit difficult?

Shall you not pray:

☦ Lord, make me willing to obey the promptings and leadership of the Holy Spirit.

- ✝ Lord, grant that I'll be sensitive to His urges, constrains, restrains, prompting etc.
- ✝ Lord, cause me to be malleable in the hands of the Holy Spirit.

You see, the prayers above are because we must be willing to follow and to obey for God says *"my spirit will not contend with man forever"* (Genesis 6:3).

There will be times when the Holy Spirit will speak and we'll not hear, when He will point but we'll not look due to lack of sensitivity, so we must pray for sensitivity; The Bible says *"you do not have because you not ask"*. Thirdly, there'll be moments when we'll get it yet be slow or stiff-necked, so we need to pray for malleability and flexibility in the hands of the Holy Spirit.

May be you should pause for a moment and thank the Holy Spirit for His guidance and direction. Thank Him for being patient with you all this while.

Now Born of God

What does it mean to be *"born of God"*?

This simply means being born again – accepting Jesus as your personal Lord and Savior, experiencing deliverance from sin and receiving a deposit of the life of God in you i.e. eternal life.

"…for everyone born of God overcomes the world …who is he that overcomes the world? Only he who believes that Jesus is the Son of God" (1 John 5:4). From this, we may conclude that, he who is born of God is he who believes that Jesus is the Son of God, with all that accompanies this. There're other phrases like *"Born of the Spirit"* (John 3:8c), *"Born of water and of the Spirit"* (John 3:5). They all mean being born again.

If you've genuinely repented of your sins and invited Jesus into your life as your personal Lord and Savior, then you have been born of God, for *"everyone who believes that Jesus is the Christ is born of God"* (1 John 5:1).

This means that you have inherited the very nature of God. You are not an ordinary man or woman. You have the deposit or better still the genes of God in you. You have inherited all of God's potentials and abilities and here on earth you can begin partaking in the divine nature. You can declare things and they come to pass, you can speak things into existence. That is what you have become by being born again.

A New Creation

> *"Therefore, if anyone is in Christ, he is a new creation; the old has gone, the new has come!"* (2 Corinthians 5:17)

Why? Because if anyone is in Christ, the old values, choices, priorities, practices are all gone and a totally new set of values, priorities, motivation and choices have come in. Everything about the person changes, his immediate company, his records in Gods books etc. A consequence of this new creation is that, there's a total change of kingdoms. The Bible talks of a transfer from one kingdom to another.

> *"He rescued us from the power of darkness and brought us safe into the kingdom of his dear Son"* (Colossians 1:13, GNT).

You see, it's a whole matter of a change of kingdoms: ruler, spirit, course, ways, principles, values and methods of the old kingdom pass away and a new set, that of the new kingdom is pursued. Have you experienced this change of kingdoms? In praying for His disciples, on that dark night of His arrest, Jesus said *"I have revealed you to those whom you gave me out to the world"* (John 17:6a). A man who is saved is one who has come out of the world, abandoned all that has to do with that system of things and thinking, has totally embraced the ways of God, and is in a dynamic relationship with God.

> *"If the world hates you, keep in mind that it hated me first. If you belonged to the world, it would love you as its own. As it is, you do not belong to the world, but I have chosen you out of the world. That is why the world hates you"* (John 15:18,19).

This change in kingdoms will not be welcomed by all around you. In fact anyone who changes kingdoms will experience an immense hatred and opposition from those around him, most probably from those to whom he was closest, when in the other kingdom. You know why? The rulers, spirits, values, ways etc. of both kingdoms are at war and consequently the children of both kingdoms will be at war. They'll spare no effort to seduce you to turn your back to Christ. In fact when you begin to face opposition, then truly you've had a change of kingdoms and I promise you, Satan will spare no effort to get you back into his kingdom. But do not fret; Jesus said of His own *"no one can snatch them out of my hand"* (John 10:28).

This brings us to the main theme of our discussion. Until now, we've tried to prepare the ground and lay the foundation of all what will be said from now onwards. As a summary, we've learned that:

1. Each individual belongs to one of two kingdoms – God's or Satan's.
2. Your citizenship is determined by your values, choices, ways, principles etc.
3. Citizenship in God's kingdom is gotten only by faith in Jesus Christ.
4. The only legitimate kingdom is God's own kingdom and Satan's kingdom will be destroyed.
5. He who is in Christ is one who has experienced a change of kingdoms from Satan's to God's, since by nature we all belong to Satan's kingdom.

Now the rest of the book is for those who are children of God. Now we shall talk of you as a child of God.

Chapter 4

Child of God

As a child of God, you have an inheritance, privileges and responsibilities, which God has ordained for you. In this section, we shall seek to study just these, and see how we can better live as children of God.

The Child's Inheritance

There is infinitely much we receive as children of God, during regeneration i.e. as a consequence of the new birth. Here, we treat a few of them, may be as I would term them, the *"outstanding"* ones.

The Peace of the Child

> *"So Gideon built an altar to the LORD there and called it The LORD is Peace"* (Judges 6:24a).

> *"For to us a child is born, to us a son is given, and the government will be on his shoulders. And he will be called Wonderful Counselor, Mighty God, Everlasting Father, Prince of Peace"* (Isaiah 9:6).

He is Jehovah Shalom – the Lord my peace, He is the Prince of peace, and *"He Himself is our peace"* (Ephesians 2:14). Every child of God has as inheritance peace from the Father. He is your peace at all times and everywhere. In times of trials, persecution, in times when all around seems to be against you, God is your peace. Besides, our Savior is the Prince of Peace. As far as Peace is concerned He is the best. None can compare and none can be compared to Him. He's the giver of peace. Something more, He is your peace. He said, *"Peace I leave with you; my peace I give you. I do not give to you as the world gives. Do not let your hearts be troubled and do not be afraid"* (John 14:27).

Our Lord has given us peace, and only in Him can our peace be found. No matter how you struggle, the world or the things in this world will never give you peace. The way peace is viewed in the kingdom is different from the way the world views peace. Kingdom peace is given in a different measure, gotten in different way, found in a different source, and its channels are different from those of this world. Let me tell you one truth: what the world calls peace, is not peace at all. The Bible says that:-

"'There is no peace,' says the LORD, 'for the wicked'" (Isaiah 48:22).

This is not a conditional statement; it is true at all times anywhere. The sinner has no peace: whether the most primitive or the most sophisticated sinner. Why? Because sin leads only to inner unrest! Everything is uncertain about the sinner. No matter how outwardly strong and courageous he appears, in the inside he's full of anxiety and fear. There's no peace for the wicked, and there's no peace in wickedness. Have you ever sinned as a child of God and then have your mind troubled until the sin is confessed and forsaken? That just shows you there is no peace in sin.

Well the wicked have no peace but the child has peace and peace in abundance. But why is it that very few of God's children experience this peace which has been given, like any other gift of God, without measure? May be the question one should ask is where does this peace live? How can I get it?

The peace of the child of God lies in number of factors:

1. Obedience

> *"If only you had paid attention to my commands, your peace would have been like a river, your righteousness like the waves of the sea" (Isaiah 48:18).*

Peace like a river – abundant peace. You see, the peace of the child depends on paying attention to the commands of God. Until there's a commitment in the heart of a child of God to obey the Lord in everything, he will know no peace. For a disobedient child of God, nothing awaits you but inner unrest and misery. Why? Because your peace lies in obedience! If such peace – abundant peace is just at our door, then why don't we get it? Here we are, with broken hearts, broken heads, in one depression after the other because, always we want to have our way, we want to do our own thing. Will you shun the way of disobedience and rebellion to God? Will you close that door totally?

> *"Why should you be beaten anymore? Why do you persist in rebellion? Your whole head is injured, your whole heart afflicted. From the sole of your foot to the top of your head there is no soundness-- only wounds and welts and open sores, not cleansed or bandaged or soothed with oil"* (Isaiah 1:5,6).

My brother, my sister, anyone who persists in rebellion will know nothing but affliction, and wounds. Please I say it from my little experience. In moments when I've resisted God in one thing or the other, I tell you it has been endless war within, emptiness and pain until there is submission. It is for this reason that the hymn writer says:

> *Perfect submission*
> *All is at rest*

Do you want to know inner rest? Then perfectly submit because, *"Great peace have they who love your law, and nothing can make them stumble"* (Psalm 119:165). There's great peace in obedience. For what does love for His law mean but to joyfully obey His word.

2. Righteousness

"Love and faithfulness meet together; righteousness and peace kiss each other" (Psalm 88:10).

Righteousness and peace are tied together, they are non-separable, they embrace each other. It means where there is righteousness, there is peace and vice versa. Is it not why the Bible says there's no peace for the wicked? The peace of the child depends on doing what is right at any particular time. Those who choose the wrong way always realize there's no peace. There's no peace in doing your brother wrong, no matter what he has done. This leads us to the third point.

3. Forgiveness

If you'll learn to forgive anyone who wrongs you, no matter what, then your peace will truly be like a river. Have you realized that each time you have something against somebody, there's no true inner peace? You begin to burn with hatred and revenge in the inside and God begins to point at it each time you come in His presence or each time you are conscious of Him? There's nothing left but to let go and forgive that individual.

4. Repentance

On the other hand, our peace lies too in God's forgiveness. Each time you have a sense of guilt you realize there is no peace within but when you become conscious of God's forgiveness, no matter what you've done, His peace floods your soul. If you want to know peace in your Christian walk, keep short records of sin i.e. be always willing to confess your sin to God.

5. Trust

"You will keep in perfect peace him whose mind is steadfast, because he trusts in you" (Isaiah 26:3).

Why is there such inner unrest, such worry, such anxiety and such uncertainty, even amongst God's children? I believe the one reason is lack of trust. This lack of trust causes us to try to know what the future holds for us, this lack of trust causes us to ask *"will I make heaven?" "Will I stand this trial?" "Will I go through this temptation?"* All this stems from nothing but the lack of trust.

If you learn to trust God at all times, and in all things, as your loving Father, One who holds a bright future for you, One who works everything for your good, One who will let no harm come your way, One who will meet your every need, then He shall keep you in perfect peace. Set your mind steadfastly on God, unmoved by the trials and temptations that come your way. To be steadfast means not changing in your attitude or aims. Thus he who is steadfast i.e. one whose attitudes to God and the things of God remain unchanging even in times of greatest difficulties, whose aim in the things of God remains unchanging, is kept in God's perfect peace. Do you realize the times you worry or are anxious about anything are times when your trust in God is shaky? If you do not trust, then you cannot be steadfast, let alone have peace.

In conclusion remember Christ Himself is our peace. As you let Him take possession of your heart, so He fills that heart with peace. In other words, your peace depends on your God content-how much of God you have in you. Do not seek peace in the world by compromising in one way or the other. This world holds nothing but trouble for any child of God. Take heart! As you trust God, no matter what happens, He'll keep you in perfect peace. Our peace lies in no other place but Christ.

CHAPTER 5

THE GRACE OF THE CHILD

What is grace?

Grace, therefore, is that unmerited favor of God towards fallen man whereby, for the sake of Christ – the only begotten of the Father, full of grace and truth (John 1:14) – He has provided for man's redemption. He has from all eternity determined to extend favor towards all who have faith in Christ as Lord and Savior. (New International Dictionary of the Bible J.D Douglas and Merrill C. Tenney, Zondervan).

The Grace that Saved You

> *"But because of his great love for us, God, who is rich in mercy, made us alive with Christ even when we were dead in transgressions--it is by grace you have been saved"* (Ephesians 2:4,5).

Do you remember how you were dead in your sins, separated from God? Do you remember how you once lived in hostility towards God? *"Think of what you were before you were saved"*. What does it look like now? But for the grace of God, we all would be lost and doomed for destruction, but grace came running after us, past our failures and shortcomings, to the point of our need–forgiveness. Grace brought to you God's forgiveness; it brought to you God's love,

His mercy and compassion. Grace opened your eyes to behold Christ in His majesty and glory; grace showed you your hopelessness and helplessness without a Savior. Grace broke the chains that kept you bound to sin, the flesh and the world. Without Christ, there's no grace and only in Him can you find grace. It didn't come as a result of your desire, your effort, but by the sovereign choice of God.

> *"It does not, therefore, depend on man's desire or effort, but on God's mercy"* (Romans 9:16).

That's why God says *"I will have mercy on whom I have mercy, and I will have compassion on whom I have compassion"* (Romans 9:15).

The package grace brought is so big that we shall continue to enjoy its contents even right to eternity. The work of grace began even before existence. Look at the process through which grace unfolded:

> *"For those God foreknew he also predestined to be conformed to the likeness of his Son, that he might be the firstborn among many brothers. And those he predestined, he also called; those he called, he also justified; those he justified, he also glorified"* (Romans 8:29-31).

- What did you do so God would foreknow you?
- What did you do so He would predestine you?
- What did you do for Him to have called you out of the mess in which you once lived?
- What did you do in order to be justified?
- What did you do to be changed from an object of God's wrath to an object of His glory?

Absolutely nothing! And there's nothing you can ever do to repay Him.

There're some who think salvation comes as a result of works of righteousness. This is not so, we're saved only because of Jesus Christ and nothing else. (Ephesians 2:8)

Grace – Abundant Grace

> *"In him we have redemption through his blood, the forgiveness of sins, in accordance with the riches of God's grace that he lavished on us with all wisdom and understanding"* (Ephesians 1:7,8).

I like the word lavish; it seems to point out the extent to which you and I have been given grace – measureless grace. This grace is unconditional, and is found only in Christ. The grace of God is inexhaustible; in eternity we shall continue to enjoy the merits of grace.

A wedding ceremony took place in our local church in Buea, during a period when power failure was very frequent all over the nation. In that wedding, I was the chief protocol. When it was time for photographs with the couple, I had to announce the order of snapshots. Unfortunately, there was not much time as darkness was fast approaching, so one of the elders of the local church told me to hurry up because *"God's grace with respect to electricity supply will soon be exhausted"*. What he meant was that, God might have *"smiled enough"* over our waste of time, and so was ready to permit power failure if we didn't stop the couple from taking photographs so the guest could go and eat. My point of narrating this story is to point out that unlike many other things, God's grace remains infinite. God's grace to us in spite of our failures, is inexhaustible, in fact it is becoming increasingly abundant.

> *"And God is able to make all grace abound to you, so that in all things at all times, having all that you need, you will abound in every good work"*
> (2 Corinthians 9:8).

God is able to make

- <u>all grace</u> abound to you. Not 50%, not 75%, not 80%, not 90%, not 95%, not 99%, not even 99.9%, but <u>all grace</u>–100% grace;
- so that in <u>all things,</u> not in some things, not in many things, not even in most things, but in <u>all things</u>–100%;

- at all times, not sometimes, not in times that we're strong and going along, not in times that we're full of zeal for His house, not most of the time but at all times, when we are weak and when we are strong, when we feel like continuing and we feel like giving up, His grace is there, always, everywhere .

Grace in Times of Need

"Let us then approach the throne of grace with confidence, so that we may receive mercy and find grace to help us in our time of need" (Hebrews 4:16).

God has made provision for us, to always obtain grace, especially in our time of need. His grace is there to help us face trials and temptations. His grace is there to hold your hand and lead you along the ways and paths of righteousness when the demands seem too hard. His grace is there to point to you that finished work of Christ on the cross of Calvary when you realize and recognize your inadequacies. To obtain grace, to find this grace to help us, we need to approach the Throne of Grace, where our Lord and Savior is seated, with open arms to welcome and receive us. Do you see a need? Then approach the Throne of Grace and you shall find grace to guide you, grace to support and sustain you.

Sufficient Grace

"But he said to me, 'My grace is sufficient for you, for my power is made perfect in weakness.' Therefore I will boast all the more gladly about my weaknesses, so that Christ's power may rest on me" (2 Corinthians 12:9).

God's grace is not just abundant, but it is sufficient. It is up to the task of meeting our every need. It is up to the task of taking us through the trials we shall face. It is up to the task of holding your hand in every situation and causing you to lift up your head when all around you bows to the circumstances around. It is up to task to keep you walking in white in a world full of stain that could soil you at any moment. It is up to task to make you bear a little more with that person, or that situation. God's grace will never be found wanting, it is always sufficient, always up to the task.

Grace that Teaches

We live in a generation which has taken for granted God's grace, they use it as a license to sin and all forms of levity. This generation invents new forms of abusing the grace of God! Listen to what the Bible says:

> *"For the grace of God that brings salvation has appeared to all men. It teaches us to say 'No' to ungodliness and worldly passions, and to live self-controlled, upright and godly lives in this present age"* (Titus 2:11,12).

The grace of God which brings salvation has appeared to all men, yet not all men have responded to it. Some have chosen the way of sin and condemnation. This grace which you've responded to, teaches you to say *"no"* to:

1. Ungodliness in this present age,
2. Worldly passions in this present age.

On the positive side, it teaches you to live:

1. A self-controlled life in this present age
2. Upright and godly lives in this present age.

Grace Teaches us to Say "No"

Increasingly, the world invents ways of doing evil and of living in rebellion towards God. Godlessness in all its form is on the rise and the righteous souls of God's elect face increasing pressure from without to join the stream. So much calls for the attention of God's children in other to lure them away from the center of their focus – Jesus Christ. Thanks to the grace God has given us which teaches us to say *"no"* to all that offends God and is unprofitable to us. No matter the pressure we face from the world and its passions, God's grace teaches God's child to say *"no"* to them.

I wonder whether those who hide under the umbrella of God's grace in order to pursue the worldly passions and pleasures, have received this grace which teaches us to say *"no"* to such things, or maybe they received some other grace which spurs them up to hide under the canopy of "grace" to commit all forms of indecency and sensuality. May be the grace they received is one which approves godlessness and encourage people to love and cherish their sin. To those obviously the grace they claim they received is far from being God's grace.

Grace Teaches us to Live

Grace teaches us to live self-controlled lives in a world where almost everything is out of control. It teaches us to live upright lives in a world where integrity is the last virtue to be found. It teaches us to live godly lives in an environment marked by all forms of ungodliness. Grace teaches you all these *"so that you may become blameless and pure, children of God without fault in a crooked and depraved generation, in which you shine like stars in the universe"* (Philippians 2:15).

Yes we live in a dishonest and morally bankrupt generation. A generation in which moral decadence has reached its climax! But grace teaches us to live and model our lives in the footsteps of He whom we are to follow. It teaches us to live pure, holy and decent lives, so that at the end, those who accuse us will find no reason or cause to blame us.

A response to grace implies a call to integrity and honesty in all forms and in everything. Have you ever thought of the standard the world places on God's children? Those who have a little knowledge of God's holiness expect Christians to be the most honest people, and that's what we should be for the grace of God is there to teach us all this. Grace teaches us how we can please God in our choices and daily decisions.

Before we round off this section, permit me ask you some very personal questions:

- Are you committed to truth and integrity?
- Are you honest and transparent in the things you do?
- Have you resolved to consistently say *"no"* to the pressures from the world?

Chapter 6

The Hope of the Child

"To them God has chosen to make known among the Gentiles the glorious riches of this mystery, which is Christ in you, the hope of glory" (Colossians 1:27).

The one hope of the child of God is Christ in him. It is not just the source of our hope but it is our hope and our comfort. All around you may fail and crumble, dreams may fade but the one hope you have is *"Christ in you the hope of glory"*. The hope of a new day in your life; the hope of *"another life"*; the hope to see Him as He is, in splendor, holiness, majesty and glory; the hope to worship at His feet; the hope of having your tears wiped by Him. If you allow this hope to fill your heart, it will lift up your head in the midst of trials and difficulties.

Hope Beyond this Life

"If only for this life we have hope in Christ, we are to be pitied more than all men" (1 Corinthians 15:19).

This hope is unique to those who truly have found Christ. They hope for a life beyond time – a life with Jesus in eternity. No other group has any *"legal"* basis to claim this hope. You know we the Christian folks have decided to abandon much because they end only in this life and not beyond, since we have hope for another life which possesses our interest. One thing I want you to know is that, sin has some pleasure, though passing and temporary.

> *"He chose to be mistreated along with the people of God rather than to enjoy the pleasures of sin for a short time. He regarded disgrace for the sake of Christ as of greater value than the treasures of Egypt, because he was looking ahead to his reward"* (Hebrews 11:25, 26).

Every child of God has refused to take part in the passing pleasures of sin and all it offers. We've refused to enjoy these things because we have a hope beyond this life. The same hope which Moses had is the hope we too have. Truly, if only for this life we have hope, we are to be the most pitied of all men, even the most miserable. We live in a world where selfish gain and ambition is the driving force; people manipulate others and things for their personal gain; no opportunity to make life better is left to pass, no matter what it involves. But for the Christian, the doors to all these are closed because we hope for another life where all things will be ours. We shall manipulate or cheat no one yet all things will be ours.

Hope for a New Home

> *"In my Father's house are many rooms; if it were not so, I would have told you. I am going there to prepare a place for you. And if I go and prepare a place for you, I will come back and take you to be with me that you also may be where I am"* (John 14:2,3).

Christian history is marked by thousands of saints who as far as a home in this life is concerned were regarded homeless. In the present time, in some lands, many have been driven out of home because of their faith, others have had their homes burned down and destroyed, others rejected by their families because of their faith, others have lost all they acquired over years of hard labor in a minute because of their confession of Christ. They move about in streets homeless, with hardly any shelter. What is it that keeps them going in the faith? Nothing but hope of another home! A home we shall share with our

Savior and Lord and all His saints. A home where all the members shall be in one accord!

Are you homeless? Is your home divided because of your profession of Christ? Do not despair; set your hope on Christ, the builder of a new home for you. The Bible talks of those who *"wandered in deserts and mountains and in caves and holes in the ground"*. You are not alone; you are in the footsteps of the heroes of faith. When you feel homeless, remind yourself that you have another home in view, which your Savior is preparing for you and He shall come and take you there as soon as He is through, and yours shall be an everlasting joy. You shall for all eternity rejoice that you went about homeless for the sake of Christ and forever you shall be amazed at the goodness of our God.

Hope to See Him

> *"Dear friends, now we are children of God, and what we will be has not yet been made known. But we know that when he appears, we shall be like him, for we shall see him as he is"* (I John 3:2).

Nothing inspires like the hope to see the One of whom the whole of scriptures speaks about. When He appears, *"we shall see Him as He is"*, no disguise. We shall see Him as the *"Lamb that was slain"*, as the *"Lion of Judah"* who reigns eternally, we shall see Him as the *"Ancient of Days"*. We all shall be amazed at His beauty, His holiness, His splendor, His majesty. We shall be amazed at His gracefulness and meekness.

Are you filled with longing to see Him? There's hope! One day you shall see Him as He is and His awesome presence shall envelop you, the beauty of His glory will surround you round about. Something greater, we shall not just see Him, but seeing Him will change us into His likeness, for *"when He appears, we shall be like Him"*. In His splendor; in His holiness, in His beauty, His majesty, His meekness, His gracefulness and purity. Like Him, we shall become immortal, for *"we shall live with Him forever"*. In fact, the whole world shall be astonished at His appearing. For us, children of God, it shall be a time of rejoicing and of running towards our Savior but for the lost, it shall be a time when all those who live in rebellion will try to flee from His presence. Even the sky and the heavenly bodies shall flee from His presence. Unfortunately there'll be no hiding place for the sinner, for the glory of the Lord will fill every corner of this universe.

Hope that Produces Faith and Love

> *"the faith and love that spring from the hope that is stored up for you in heaven and that you have already heard about in the word of truth"*
> (Colossians 1:5).

The source of faith is hope. As you set your hope on Christ and the things above you will realize a new sense of faith in your Christian life. There'll be faith that the things you desire shall happen, the things you ask will be given. Hope gives birth to faith in God and in His promises even in the most trying moments. To grow in faith, grow in hope. If you ask anyone whose faith diminished, you'll find this drop in faith to have resulted from a drop in hope or worse still a change in the object of their hope. Anyone who abandons the Way to run after worldly things has transferred his hope in God to hope in wealth and personal accomplishments. That is why Paul wrote to Timothy:

> *"Command those who are rich in this present world not to be arrogant nor to put their hope in wealth, which is so uncertain, but to put their hope in God, who richly provides us with everything for our enjoyment"*
> (I Timothy 6:17).

If your hope is in God, you will realize a deep sense of meaninglessness of wealth and this will produce in you a spirit of sacrifice and generosity; a compelling willingness to share with those in need.

Hope in God delivers from a spirit of hoarding. Hope in God produces trust and confidence that there's something better. It will stir you up to meet the needs of your fellow brother or sister, and even the needs of the sinner. You see, God wants to reach the world through you and me but unless our hope rest entirely on Him, we shall not truly love the world for which His Son died so as to sacrifice all we do not need, in meeting the needs of others. No one can put His hope in God and wealth and live an effective and a productive Christian life.

Hope that Anchors

> *"God did this so that, by two unchangeable things in which it is impossible for God to lie, we who have fled to take hold of the hope offered to us may be greatly encouraged. We have this hope as an anchor for the soul, firm and secure. It enters the inner sanctuary behind the curtain" (Hebrews 6:18-19).*

> *"…a better hope is introduced, by which we draw near to God" (Hebrews 7:19b).*

Our hope is the anchor of the soul in this sea of the Christian life. Hope keeps us from drifting in the sea of life. It is a firm and secure anchor for the soul. Without it you cannot effectively move forward towards the harbor of heaven. It is hope that takes you nearer God, in devotion and commitment, in fellowship and service. Without hope there is no way you can draw near to the throne of God. Hope is what gives you access into the holy of holies – the inner sanctuary where Christ entered on our behalf. Without it you remain in the outer courts, deprived of the things which can only be gotten by those who with confidence approach the Throne room of the King of the universe.

Immediately anyone loses hope he begins to drift about in the sea of life without purpose and direction. Such a person drifts into the whirl waters of confusion and frustration. Hope should be taken hold of; it is your link and connection into the Throne room. When your hope has entered the Throne room, you immediately have access to all that is within it. You have an anchor my dear, do not leave it inside your vessel, take it and throw it into the solid rock and the raging waters of life will not set you adrift!

The Responsibility of Hope

1. Hope Demands Purity

> *"Dear friends, now we are children of God, and what we will be has not yet been made known. But we know that when he appears, we shall be like him, for we shall see him as he is. Everyone who has this hope in him purifies himself, just as he is pure"* (I John 3:2,3).

The hope of seeing Christ Jesus in the beauty of His holiness is no ordinary hope. It is not a hope without implication. To better put it, it is hope that imposes a lot of responsibility on those who possess it. Take for an example that you receive an invitation to the presidency, imagine your initial reaction and the preparation which accompanies your hope of seeing the president and chatting with him. Do you see how much you'll put in the preparation as concerns your appearance? The aroma which will come from the perfume you'll wear? The smile you labor to put on?

Thus your hope of meeting the president brought in some responsibility. In the same light, every child of God has the hope to see the King of the universe, the God of all creation, the One who is our very life and who is for all eternity. The responsibility of this hope is not our physical appearance but that of the soul, the purity of the heart. It is to this John is calling every child of God, to put away all that contaminates the soul, purify our motives and thoughts.

There are many who in the light of God's word have a false hope. They hope to, one day, see the Savior yet do nothing to live pure lives. They refuse to keep themselves from being "polluted by the world" – its values, principles, ways, offers etc. Do you have hope? That hope demands purity. It is for this same reason that our Lord said only the pure in heart shall see God. The privilege of seeing the holy God is given only to those who have assumed hope's responsibility to keep their hearts pure.

> *"Blessed are the pure in heart, for they will see God"* (Matthew 5:8).

It is a blessing to be pure in heart. This blessing, I believe, is that you'll see God, not only when He comes but even in this life, you'll see Him manifested in every domain of your life, as you labor to walk with Him in purity. Purity has an added blessing of keeping communion with God uninterrupted.

2. Hope Demands Obedience

> *"But in keeping with his promise we are looking forward to a new heaven and a new earth, the home of righteousness. So then, dear friends, since you are looking forward to this, make every effort to be found spotless, blameless and at peace with him"* (2 Peter 3:13-14).

If you read the whole of 2 Peter 3, there are things which came out about our hope:

- hope of *"the day of the Lord"*
- hope for a new home, *"the home of righteousness".*

Like John, Peter brings out the responsibility of the believer as a result of this blessed hope that each one of us has. If we had no hope for the coming of our Savior and of us being partakers in the *"home of righteousness"* then we may afford to live the way we want, how it seems pleasing to our human nature and its cravings. Peter says this hope we have compels us to labor i.e. to *"make every effort"*. In other words, he commands us to put in every bit of our physical, mental, and spiritual energy to be

1. Spotless
2. Blameless
3. At peace with God

No matter how difficult or demanding it may be, spare no energy, spare nothing whatsoever to ensure the above.

Spotlessness talks of being without sin, living a sin-free life. I belief this is possible, for God will not call us to do the impossible. Blamelessness, talks of being without defects in our character. It is a call for you to labor to put on the character of Christ. It gives no ground for accusing spirits to accuse you before your heavenly Father. Remember the account of Joshua the high Priest (Zechariah 3). Being at peace with God demands obedience. Remember we said the peace of the child of God depends largely on obedience. Hope calls you indirectly, through peace to render obedience to God in all things.

Beyond what Hope Can Measure

> *"No eye has seen, no ear has heard, no mind has conceived what God has prepared for those who love him" (I Corinthians 2:9).*

One thing is sure; we always try to picture what is in store for us. We try to imagine the surprises we are going to have on *"the day of the Lord"*. No matter what we hope for, God has prepared something greater, higher, deeper, and more than what we can hope for. What we shall see and receive will be far beyond the limit of our hope. How great, how gracious, how loving, how caring is our heavenly Father who has prepared for us, things we can never conceive as at now.

No matter how much knowledge of these things we may have received, even from the Word, I strongly believe, as the Bible says, *"now we know in part, then we shall know in full"*. Have you ever stood on the shore of the Atlantic Ocean? You see how vast it is, how it stretches far beyond the limits your normal eyes can measure. At best you can only estimate its vastness. That is how limited the hope you have can estimate what heaven has kept in store for you. That which your hope has revealed to you is nothing compared to that which is beyond hope's capacity to measure.

Chapter 7

The Child's Freedom

Freedom for humanity was bought more than 2.000 years ago on the cross of Calvary, when Jesus *"the Lamb of God who takes away the sin of the world"* was slain. On the cross He cried out that *"it is finished"*. What was finished? His mission on planet earth was finished. Do you remember what His mission was? For a little reminder, turn with me to Luke 4:18;19

> *"The Spirit of the Lord is on me, because he has anointed me to preach good news to the poor. He has sent me to proclaim freedom for the prisoners and recovery of sight for the blind, to release the oppressed, to proclaim the year of the Lord's favor" (Luke 4:18-19).*

From this, five things can readily be pointed out as part of His mission, which He told the Father *"I have brought you glory on earth by completing the work you gave me to do"* (John 17:4).

1. To preach the goodnews to the poor
2. To proclaim freedom for prisoners
3. To proclaim recovery of sight for the blind
4. To release the oppress
5. To proclaim the year of the Lord's favor.

In this section, we'll dwell on the accomplishment of points 2 and 4 which talk of freedom for prisoners and release of the oppressed. The question one may ask is why so many in the world are still bound to the law of sin and death? Bondage to Satan and his influences, bondage to wrong habits and addictions! Why are many still under the oppression of the evil one and his host? Well the answer to this is simple and clear. Those who reject His Salvation reject all that comes in God's big unmerited package.

The work of the cross can only be made true in the lives of those who respond to the love of our God and His Christ. Freedom from sin and slavery to Satan was accomplished on the cross for each one who responds to God's love. Yet not all are free, why? There are three reasons, I believe, why some of God's children are still bound by one thing or another:-

1. They lack knowledge of their freedom
2. They cherish the thing that keeps them bound
3. Satan is making false claims.

Lack of Knowledge of Freedom

This lack of knowledge of the accomplishment of the cross of Calvary plagued the early church in Galatia. They were still, kind of, bound by an obligation to obey the Jewish customs and traditions. In other words they felt obliged to live according to the customs passed down to them from generation to generation especially the custom of circumcision.

The problem current day believers face with respect to their freedom will obviously be different from that of circumcision. We find even in many born again religious circles rules like: thou shall not touch, thou shall not do this, and thou shall not do that. Many who have been set free are brought into bondage in the very place where they were to obtain freedom. They forget to know that in Christ *"the only thing that counts is faith expressing itself through love"* (Galatians 5:6). Have you not seen many who are bound by valueless rules and regulations? When laws are made apart from the clearly revealed divine principles in scripture, then the grace of Christ is gradually being kept aside. Why do so many believe in laws as though we are saved through laws? It is clear that anyone who wants to get on with Christ must model his life through some principles to which he abides; for him they may act as checks or even a spring board to excellence, but once they are forced on another person, it becomes laws without basis and the soul Christ came to set free is again entangled in rules of human tradition.

Well, the Bible reveals the moral will of God in all aspects of life and if you're in a dynamic relationship with God, His Spirit will guide you in the understanding of God's will with respect to many things in life. Search the scriptures and allow God to speak to your heart. Remember we're talking of the freedom brought to us by Christ, as a result of the finished work of the cross of Calvary. He told the Jews on this subject:

> ... *"I tell you the truth, everyone who sins is a slave to sin.* [35] *Now a slave has no permanent place in the family, but a son belongs to it forever. So if the Son sets you free, you will be free indeed"* (John 8:34-36).

Is there any sin in your life which you know you're bound to? Any sin still demands that you be its slave? Any habit you feel trapped in? As time passes you still find yourself increasingly tormented by this sin, no matter how small it may appear. Like Lazarus you have the life of Christ in you but you're still bound by the grave clothes of the life to which you died. If this is your case I counsel you to go to some spiritual authority, expose things to him and pray together, so that you can indeed enter your freedom whether from sin, or from some wrong habits or from oppression by enemy forces. In Christ you are a free being, indebted to no one but Christ alone who paid your debt and broke your every chain. Declare your freedom to the hearing of the devil and his hosts, remind him if need be of the victory on the cross of Calvary over his works. No matter what, in the words of Apostle Paul *"stand firm, then and do not let yourself be burdened again by a yoke of slavery"*.

Read and meditate on passages like Romans 6, Romans 8 and Galatians 5.

Knowledge brings freedom. Imagine a prisoner who has been set free, yet has not got the news of his freedom. He will remain in prison, especially when he who keeps guard is cruel so as to hide the news from the prisoner, until he gets the knowledge that he has been set free. It is this knowledge with which you shall be enlightened by the Spirit of God as you meditate on those passages and allow the Spirit of grace to minister to your soul.

Cherishing the thing that keeps you bound

The second group of those still bound is those who cherish the things that keep them bound. It may be sin, wrong habits or satanic oppression. It is as though they've made a covenant with Satan so as to remain in hiding, never willing to bring to light the torments their poor souls are subjected to. Even when brought to light, you must be willing to be set free, you must denounce every practice which gives a legal ground for your soul to be kept bound. Remember we have a God who respects spiritual principles. Unless you denounce or renounce your allegiance to the thing that keeps you bound, you shall in no way receive your freedom especially when you have knowledge. May be the passage of scripture in Exodus 21 will help you understand what I'm trying to put forth.

> *"If you buy a Hebrew servant, he is to serve you for six years. But in the seventh year, he shall go free, without paying anything…But if the servant declares, 'I love my master and my wife and children and do not want to go free,' then his master must take him before the judges. He shall take him to the door or the doorpost and pierce his ear with an awl. Then he will be his servant for life"* (Exodus 21:2,5,6).

You see, your freedom to an extent depends on whether you accept to be set free or you give what keeps you bound a greater command over your poor soul. Such is the case of many who refuse to acknowledge certain habits as sinful thereby getting themselves in greater bondage and service to the enemy. The Lord Jesus has proclaimed your freedom, accept it and begin to live in the freedom. You do not have to pay a penny. As you acknowledge His Lordship the claims which have tormented your poor soul will be broken, for *"if the Son sets you free you shall be free indeed"*.

Satan is making false claims

The third group of those still living in bondage are those who have the knowledge of their freedom, hate what keeps them bound, yet they find themselves in slavery to it as all attempts to set themselves free has failed. Satan is making false claims over their souls. S.D. Gordon in his book *"Quiet talks on prayer"* said there're six facts which underlie prayer, the sixth being that Satan has been defeated but:-

1. he refuses to acknowledge his defeat
2. he refuses to surrender his dominion until he must– he yields only what he must when he must.
3. He is supported in his ambition by man
4. He hopes yet to make his possession of the earth permanent.

You see, what we're saying is that, freedom for the world has been bought on the cross and Satan has no right whatsoever to claim ownership to anything, let alone the soul which Christ inhabits. Yet in most cases, he refuses to acknowledge his defeat and continues to make false claims over innocent souls. Those who refuse to acknowledge Christ are supporting Satan in his selfish ambitions. His plans are geared towards making his possession of many a soul permanent but thank God Christ Jesus is there to set free from captivity and bondage, those who'll acknowledge His Name.

One thing is clear: Satan will refuse you your freedom until he is forced to quit. That is why the Lord Jesus Christ talks of casting out or expelling demons. They must be compelled to leave and do so permanently by the authority handed to us the saints by the glorious Lord Jesus Christ, who was slain and rose again victoriously. This calls for watchfulness and prayer on the part of the saints on behalf of the captives. Through prayer, you shall drive away the enemy and obtain your freedom. Your joker in this warfare to liberate your soul is the death and resurrection of Christ and His eternal defeat of Satan and evil. Remember he yields only what he must when he must.

The Other Side of Freedom

The death of Jesus Christ on the cross of Calvary was not only to bring us freedom from sin, from sinful habits and from Satan and his hosts. There is another side of freedom which Christ has brought us into. No one can claim this freedom on his own, it is only through Christ and in Christ that this freedom, like the other side we just discussed, is obtained.

1. **Freedom to Ask**

    "And I will do whatever you ask in my name, so that the Son may bring glory to the Father. You may ask me for anything in my name, and I will do it" (John 14:13,14).

    "If you remain in me and my words remain in you, ask whatever you wish, and it will be given you" (John 15:7).

    "In that day you will no longer ask me anything. I tell you the truth, my Father will give you whatever you ask in my name. Until now you have not asked for anything in my name. Ask and you will receive, and your joy will be complete" (John 16:23,24).

There's one word which characterizes these three quotations from scripture. The word is *"whatever"* or according to the New Century Version of the Bible, *"anything"*. It is the child's freedom to ask the Father for anything, anywhere anytime. It says you can ask without limitation. God does not lay any emphasis on the kind of things you should ask. Like a little child, ask Him of the things you need, ask Him of the things you want to know, ask Him of your privileges as a child so as to explore them to the fullest. Ask Him of the things you have doubts about, the things you are uncertain of. Ask His help in times of need, ask His forgiveness when you offend Him, ask Him to fulfill His promise to you, ask Him for the salvation of your loved ones. The sphere is yours to determine, the limit is yours to determine, the time is yours to determine, the place is yours to determine. Remember it is asking for anything and not some things. How great is our God and Father, to give us such liberty. Won't you bless His holy Name for such generosity?

2. Freedom to Approach

> *"In him and through faith in him we may approach God with freedom and confidence"* (Ephesians 3:12).

> *"Let us then approach the throne of grace with confidence, so that we may receive mercy and find grace to help us in our time of need"* (Hebrews 4:16).

You see, God would have given us freedom to ask, but only to ask from a distance, without approaching Him, or His Throne of Grace. But He went beyond just giving you freedom to ask to give you freedom to approach. You are not required to ask from a distance. The freedom to approach is not just attached to when you have something to ask. It is freedom to approach (with reverence though) anytime. Approach Him for moments of discussion and dialogue, approach Him, when you need His counsel, when you need His encouragement, approach Him to receive an embrace, approach Him for words of comfort. Approach Him when you just feel like resting in the arms of your Father; His arms of love, of care and of protection. Approach Him for guidance and direction. The blood of the Lamb has made a way for you and me, without His blood having been shed on the cross, we could have no liberty to approach. Glory be to the Lord Jesus Christ!

3. Freedom to Choose

> *"Everything is permissible for me"–but not everything is beneficial. "Everything is permissible for me"–but I will not be mastered by anything"* (1 Corinthians 6:12).

> *"Everything is permissible"--but not everything is beneficial. "Everything is permissible"--but not everything is constructive"* (1 Corinthians 16:23).

For every child of God, everything is permissible, as long as it is not sin, as long as it will not lure away your soul from focusing on Christ. Anything that won't stand as a barrier between you and God is permissible. God has revealed His moral will in the Bible and every choice made within that moral will is permissible. In His generosity, He has given you a wide range of choices to make with respect to your daily life and living. Remember, though everything is permissible, not everything is beneficial and not everything is constructive. There is one principle which must guide the exercise of our freedom. It is that *"Nobody should seek his own good, but the good of others"*. This brings us to our next point:

The Responsibility of Freedom

> *"Be careful, however, that the exercise of your freedom does not become a stumbling block to the weak."* (1 Corinthians 8:9).

> *"Nobody should seek his own good, but the good of others"*
> (1 Corinthians 10:24).

Ensure that the exercise of your freedom is not a stumbling block to some other person, or that it does not prevent others from exercising their own freedom. In exercising your freedom, do those things which will build you up in the faith, those things which will strengthen others up. It is freedom to choose the things which are beneficial to us, our fellow brethren, to God and His kingdom inclusively. Exercise your freedom in such a way that the enemy won't have any ground for accusation. If your freedom is governed by these, then you shall always be on the right track. That's what it entails in having freedom to choose.

There're some who have mistaken, totally or partially, the freedom in Christ for license to sin and sensual indulgence. Such have no sense of restrain over the sinful nature and its desires.

The Child's Freedom

1. Your freedom has a limit

"You, my brothers, were called to be free. But do not use your freedom to indulge the sinful nature; rather, serve one another in love" (Galatians 5:13).

"Live as free men, but do not use your freedom as a cover-up for evil; live as servants of God" (I Peter 2:16).

Do not try to use your freedom as cover up for sin, especially rebellion. We live in an age where independence from anything called authority is on the rise, bills passed by parliaments all over the world seek to make man free from all what is called authority, be it at home, at school or at work. This is not God's purpose of freedom. Freedom in Christ does not mean you stop being accountable to your parents or to spiritual authority. Don't use your freedom to say *"No one has the right to judge me"* when your mistakes are pointed out or when confronted with your sin. The human nature is one which craves for independence. It wants to be its own master, doing things the way it wants. Putting yourself under authority will save your soul from abusing freedom.

From the two passages of scriptures above two things come out clearly.

1. Freedom demands that we serve one another in Love.
2. Freedom demands that we live as servants of God.

To conclude this section on freedom, let's summarize the main points

1. Freedom has been bought by Christ for all who call on His Name; freedom from sin, from wrong habits and from oppression by Satan.
2. Christ has given us freedom to ask anything from Him, to approach God with confidence, and freedom to choose as long as it is God's revealed will
3. Freedom has responsibilities and must be checked with respect to:
   a. Its benefits
   b. How constructive it is

And it also demands that
- c. We serve one another in love
- d. We live as servants of God. Living as servants of God implies living a life of love, peace, purity, spotlessness, blamelessness and holiness.

CHAPTER 8

THE CHILD'S VICTORY

We just talked of our freedom from the master who ruled us before we came to the saving knowledge of Christ. Though we've been set free, our former master will not allow us enjoy our freedom. They seek relentlessly through every means possible to enslave our souls set free by the Savior. Thus, day after day we find ourselves at war with enemy forces too great to overcome if ever we were left on our own. Thanks be to God, that Christ did not only buy our freedom but also won a victory for us on the cross of Calvary. It is victory won, once and for all. On the cross, Satan was defeated and his fury is aimed at every soul which enjoys and lives under the benefits of his defeat. As long as the One who defeated him is invincible, he aims his fiery ordeals at the objects of love of the Victor King. He seeks to attack and destroy the soul of the child of God through three avenues.

1. Through the deceitfulness of sin
2. Through the cravings of the flesh
3. Through the vanity of the world and all it offers.

On Calvary, Christ defeated each of these enemies to your soul. Like their master Satan, they refuse to acknowledge their defeat and so constantly wage war against God's children. Do not fret; the victory of Christ is yours, as long as you remain on the side of the Victor.

A Call to Overcome Evil

> *"Do not be overcome by evil, but overcome evil with good"* (Romans 12:21).

We live in a generation where evil in all its form and disguises come knocking persistently on the door of our hearts. Evil does not hesitate to push open any door which is not firmly closed and guarded. Once it gains access, no matter how, it seeks always and forcefully to establish its reign over the whole. Evil will seldom accept a part; it seeks invariably to take possession of the whole. Usually it comes at first in innocent but appealing ways, and seeks to gain possession through deception and presumption. If in disguise it meets a firm resistance from the soul in which Christ reigns, it never gives up and never hesitates to mobilize all its schemes and wiles to launch an open assault on that soul. Evil, be it through an open assault, through the deceitfulness of sin or through the vanity of the world keeps asking for our allegiance and partnership, through which it seeks to accomplish its goal of subduing and overcoming the soul.

The Lord, through Paul, calls us to stand our guard, wage a counter offensive and overcome this prevalent evil that surrounds us. To escape from such a fierce battle would mean leaving planet earth. Hence as long as you remain here you are called to overcome lest you be overcome. It is therefore a compulsory war for every Christian who truly calls on the Name of Christ. How can we overcome this evil? Do we just keep on resisting, watching every avenue and seeing that evil does not penetrate? As good as that is, military strategy has always proven that the camp which remains on the defensive will end up losing the war. It is for this reason that Paul calls on us to overcome evil. How? With good! That is, knowing the good you ought to do and going ahead to perform it. That's the strategy of overcoming evil. Remember we face the foe only on the basis of Christ's victory over evil.

Victory Over Sin

> *"For we do not have a high priest who is unable to sympathize with our weaknesses, but we have one who has been tempted in every way, just as we are-- yet was without sin"* (Hebrews 4:15).

The very first victory of Christ over sin is His life on earth, lived in white, without sin or fault. Like us, He lived in a society soaked in sin and faced immense temptation and assaults from the evil one, yet He was without sin or fault or blame. This led the Jews to frame false stories since they couldn't find any legal grounds to levy their charges against Him. To make this victory ours, He went to the cross that sin (my sin and yours) should be nailed to the cross and rendered powerless.

> *"Where, O death is your victory? Where, O death is your sting? The sting of death is sin, and the power of sin is the law. But thanks be to God! He gives us the victory through our Lord Jesus Christ"* (1 Corinthians 15:55-57).

The sting of death is sin, and since death has lost its victory, so has sin lost its victory over us. Daily, in your battle against sin, trust God for victory, depend on His victory. The Bible says *"He gives us victory through our Lord Jesus Christ"*. It is a continuous process of victory over sin, every second, every minute, every hour, and every day. God gives us victory over sin.

In the innermost chamber of your heart, acknowledge and proclaim this victory, and claim it daily, hourly and every moment. If you shall do this, then you'll realize His victory over sin is yours for the asking and for the living.

Victory Over the World

> *"I have told you these things, so that in me you may have peace. In this world you will have trouble. But take heart! I have overcome the world"*
> (John 16:33).

- Do you remember our definition of the world?
- Do you remember how organized the system is?

Like Satan, the world is another conquered foe who will not accept its defeat on the cross. Increasingly it struggles to establish its grip on the planet. It advances forcefully with a determination to eliminate anyone who will not abide by its system of values, ways, principles, wisdom etc. This end time will be marked by tribulation - the great tribulation during which, the world in cooperation with Satan will try to conquer every living thing on the face of the planet. Anyone who shall not pledge openly his allegiance to the world will have to pay with his life. It will be a moment of agony for all those who pledge allegiance to the Lion of Judah, but even then it shall utterly fail for it shall receive a final blow and fall to rise no more.

Do you daily feel the pressure of the world on your soul, asking and seeking its allegiance? Do you hear the persistent knocking on the door of your heart by the world with its offers of comfort, happiness, pleasure and luxury? Everything in the world demands your attention and seeks continuously to occupy a position in your heart, and unless that heart is properly guarded, the world shall never hesitate to force its way through. It is a militant world that will not shun violence if that is the only means to establish its reign over the soul.

Biblical Strategy to Overcoming the World

The world is such a powerful foe that if we were left to ourselves, the next moment will bring us nothing but defeat and we shall find ourselves bowing in allegiance to it. But thank God for the strategy to overcoming the world revealed in scripture.

Step 1: Do not Love the World

One reason why so many feel defeated already by the world is that they've failed to identify the world as an enemy to their soul. The worst enemy is the one you fail to identify or recognize as an enemy and as you allow it to get closer, it is given a greater opportunity to eliminate you without raising much alarm. This is what the world does, it offers you comfort and pleasure but its goal is to lure your soul away from the One who loves you.

He who loves the world is already defeated though apparently he may be on the Victor's side. We shall see the reasons why.

> "You adulterous people, don't you know that friendship with the world is hatred toward God? Anyone who chooses to be a friend of the world becomes an enemy of God" (James 4:4).

Firstly, the love of the world is spiritual adultery and who is that husband or wife who shall continuously tolerate adulterous acts of the partner? The thing is that, God's children take this sin so lightly without a single idea of how it pains the heart of God. Can you give your spouse a permit to commit adultery just once a year? Yet we expect God to understand us. Like any other sin, spiritual adultery makes us liable to the attack of the enemy and hence susceptible to defeat.

Secondly, the love of the world is hatred (enmity) towards God. Can you face the horror of being classified as a God-hater? Yet that's what you are if you live by the standards, philosophy, values, principles and ways of this world. All God-haters are on the camp of the evil one. Being a God-hater in God's camp can only mean you're a spy and deserve the treatment of a spy.

> "^{15} Do not love the world or the things in the world. If you love the world, the love of the Father is not in you. ^{16} These are the ways of the world: wanting to please our sinful selves, wanting the sinful things we see, and being too proud of what we have. None of these come from the Father, but all of them come from the world. ^{17} The world and everything that people want in it are passing away, but the person who does what God wants lives forever" (1 John 2:15-17, NCV).

Thirdly, loving the world is evidence of lack of love for the Father; this means you automatically forfeit all the promises of God. For God's promises and reward are for those who love Him. Do you love God? Then you cannot love the world. Do you love the world and its ways (vs 16)? Then the love of the Father is not in you.

Fourthly and lastly, since the world and all its values, desires, ways etc. are passing away, all who love it and are living by it will definitely pass away, along with the world.

Therefore to be better placed for victory over the world, do not love it, or the things in it. Someone rightly said that, though we are to use the things in the world, we are not to love them; they should occupy no place in our hearts. The heart is meant to love God only and only Jesus should occupy our heart – all of it and nothing else.

Step 2: Claim Christ's Victory (Employ Faith)

> "...For everyone born of God overcomes the world. This is the victory that has overcome the world, even our faith. Who is it that overcomes the world? Only he who believes that Jesus is the Son of God" (I John 5:4, 5).

Are you born of God? Do you believe that Jesus is the Son of God, with all its implications? Then you are the one who overcomes the world. Every new day, stand on the victory that is yours in Christ Jesus. Claim and live daily, nay, hourly your victory over the world, its system of philosophy, of viewing things, of valuing things and of viewing people. Have faith and continue to have faith in God. Your faith is indispensable for victory. Have faith that you are a victor and that you shall continue to live above the standards and values and ways and principles of the world. It has no power over you. As long as you're in Christ, it is a defeated foe that won't give up but take heart, it will be defeated again, and this time, never to rise anymore.

Victory Over Satan

> "I write to you, young men, because you have overcome the evil one. I write to you, dear children, because you have known the Father...I write to you, young men, because you are strong, and the word of God lives in you, and you have overcome the evil one" (1 John 2:13b, 14b).

Before we comment on the above scripture, remember what Jesus said to His disciples:

> "I saw Satan fall like lightning from heaven. I have given you authority to trample on snakes and scorpions and to overcome all the power of the enemy; nothing will harm you" (Luke 10:18,19).

Satan is a fallen prince, defeated even before our Savior went to the cross of Calvary. On Calvary he received his greatest blow. He's just an enemy who brags about though he knows he has no power over those in Christ. Remember what S.D Gordon said: For a reminder Satan is a defeated foe who refuses to acknowledge his defeat, he refuses to surrender his dominion and will yield only what he must when he must.

Though he knows the battle was lost by him more than 2000 years ago, he gives his subjects a wrong impression as though he is the winner of the battle. However each day, he receives defeat, again and again in the Name of the Victor from those who call on the Name of Christ. As we face the evil one, stand on the authority Christ gave you and me. Know that it is authority over all the power of the enemy. Not authority to resist all his power but authority to overcome all the power of the enemy. When he comes bragging around, remind him of the victory of the cross.

Now let's return to 1 John. Take note of the tense used in this passage. It portrays an accomplished event, *"you have overcome"*, not *"you will overcome"* or not *"you are overcoming"*. Your victory over Satan is already accomplished, all you need to do is to live in it and live it out. Though he refuses to acknowledge his defeat, he knows he has been defeated and stands defeated. There is no replay, no return fight. In the final battle, this is what the Bible says:-

> "And then the lawless one will be revealed, whom the Lord Jesus will overthrow with the breath of his mouth and destroy by the splendor of his coming" (2 Thessalonians 2:8).

Will it really be a fight? Certainly not, Satan has no strength to fight any longer; he still suffers the effect of the blow of Calvary and that of the resurrection. They were two powerful blows within seventy-two hours and though he still makes noise, he will be totally overthrown just by the breath of our Lord. Have you ever blown something with the breath of your mouth and it falls? How strong was that thing? That's just what Satan's strength measures up to before our Lord.

The Cross that Triumphed

> *"And having disarmed the powers and authorities, he made a public spectacle of them, triumphing over them by the cross"* (Colossians 2:15).

Talking about the ruler of this world in chapter one, we described Satan's system of government as the council of hell.

Christ on the cross triumphed over all of them, from Satan at the top down through principalities, powers, rulers to the host of wickedness. The Bible says He disarmed them and made a public spectacle of them. In the spirit realm, their weapons are on display. Over and over the scene of their defeat is replayed. The cross of Christ has triumphed, Hallelujah! That's why Paul could say:

> *"But thanks be to God, who always leads us in triumphal procession in Christ and through us spreads everywhere the fragrance of the knowledge of him"* (2 Corinthians 2:14).

God leads us in a triumphal procession day after day, over temptation, over sin, over the world, over the flesh, and over Satan. May we also carry our crosses to our own Calvary and make that victory real in our lives. S.D Gordon, in his book *"Quite Talks on Prayer"*, says to be a follower of Jesus means for you:

1. The wilderness; intense temptation
2. The obscure village of Nazareth; i.e. unknown.
3. The first Judean year for you – lack of appreciation
4. Desertion of friends
5. A Gethsemane
6. A Calvary

As you face each of these, remember, the One who first trod that path and called you to it is the Victor. Calvary for each one of us is the start point of our victory; do not hesitate to carry your own cross to your Calvary. On it lies the first step to victory. Remember what comes after Calvary is resurrection life.

The Child's Righteousness and Holiness

Christ Jesus has become for you and me righteousness and holiness from God. It is God who has made provision for you and me to become righteous through the atoning work of Jesus; His substitutionary death and resurrection made Him the Lord your Righteousness (1 Corinthians 1:30).

The Child's Protection

As a child of God you have access to the shelter of the protecting wings of your Lord. Live daily with the knowledge that His hand of protection is over you. He has placed at your disposal angels to watch over you and guard you. You are never alone. He is your refuge, your stronghold, your fortress, your shield and defender.

Chapter 9

The Child's Health

Another thing which was bought on the cross of Calvary is your healing. I believe good health and healing are a portion of the salvation package God, through Christ Jesus, has offered you as a result of your faith is His Son.

Every sickness or disease can be attributed to one of these causes:

1. Sin
2. Demons
3. Natural causes.

As children of God, we no longer live in slavery to sin; we do not offer the parts of our body as instruments of sin, thus disease which come as a result of sin, may not be yours. Too many diseases can be traced as a result of a curse which came to your family due to the sins of your ancestors. In Christ, such curses can be broken and the diseases which they brought along healed.

Every disease which science attributes to genetics is a result of a curse on your family line. Such curses can only be broken when sin is confessed, and then healing will follow. There're many in the family of God whom God has endowed with the authority to break such curses and set the oppressed free.

Do not hesitate to consult those who have been identified to possess such gifts. Usually, God will give them the word of wisdom to know the cause and source of the curse and sickness. We bless the Lord for giving us different gifts for the building of His church.

The second class of sickness and diseases is that caused by demons. The gospels are full of accounts of such diseases that were healed when the people were delivered. The Lord Jesus on sending out the twelve *"gave them power and authority to drive out all demons and to cure diseases"* (Luke 9:1).

I believe strongly that the order in which their operation is mentioned here matters a lot. It was first of all *"driving out demons"* then *"curing diseases"*. For diseases caused by demons, unless a complete and total deliverance is carried out, healing will never be complete. I've taken part in several deliverance sessions where people received their healing when the demons left. Pray for the gift of discernment of spirits so as to discern whether a particular disease is from a curse or from demons. Often than not, diseases which result from demonic oppression will not yield to drugs and even to prayers of healing until the demons are driven out.

The third class of diseases originate from natural causes, may be like malnutrition, mosquito bites, dirty water etc. Usually this class responds to medication and other natural methods for healing.

Whatever the class of sickness or disease, the Bible says:

> *"Is any one of you sick? He should call the elders of the church to pray over him and anoint him with oil in the name of the Lord. And the prayer offered in faith will make the sick person well; the Lord will raise him up. If he has sinned, he will be forgiven"* (James 5:14-15).

As they anoint you, and if need be carry out the necessary deliverance, you will receive your healing. If it was a result of sin, then you will also be healed as God forgives.

What then is the basis for our healing? It is found in I Peter 2:24.

> *"He himself bore our sins in his body on the tree, so that we might die to sins and live for righteousness; by his wounds you have been healed"* (1 Peter 2:24).

No matter the cause of the disease, Jesus Christ bought your healing on the cross. Is it through sin? He bore your sin on His body on the cross. Is it through a curse? He became a curse for you? You have a Father who speaks and heals every disease. He says, *"...for I am the Lord who heals you."* Irrespective of the disease, irrespective of the cause, He is Jehovah Rapha, the Lord your Healer.

Good health is yours to claim every time, every day. It is your portion in Christ, it is your inheritance. Pray for a robust body, pray for a supernatural immune system against diseases. If you are infected do not despair, there's no promise which says those in Christ will never fall ill from natural causes. If need be take drugs and pray that God will heal you through them. But remember that healing is your inheritance. Christ came to set you free from the oppression of sickness.

Just to slip in a piece of counsel here; in case you fall sick, do not just rush to a physician or to those with *"gifts of healing"* but turn first to your heavenly Father and tell Him about your sickness, then prayerfully discern the cause of the sickness. Many lives could be saved, much money and efforts and even prayers spared if the causes of diseases where discerned early enough so as to seek the appropriate method of healing. There are certain sicknesses which obviously, medicine cannot handle. For such, quietly turn to God. Better still ask Him how He likes to heal that disease then go ahead and seek your healing through that channel. Remember that the faith of the patient in some cases will be the principal factor that determines healing. So have faith and receive your healing.

Chapter 10

The Child's Privileges

The child of the modern man, usually, has much to inherit from its father when it comes to material possession, bank accounts etc. Many children have parents who meet their every need financially and materially be it at school, at home or socially.

Yet for thousands, it is luxury to spend thirty minutes daily with their parents. The embrace and comfort that comes from the loving arms of a father is far fetch. The life of many a youngster is marred by lack of parental counsel and example. Many suffer from lack of fatherly love and concern – concern about the child's upbringing, concern about the formation of inward character in the child, concern about the kind of things the child is exposed to, concern about guiding and leading the child.

Still many are being destroyed for lack of discipline due to their fathers' neglect. Where are the fathers who take time to show love and concern for their children? Where are the fathers who spend time in guiding and leading the innocent souls of their children from the evil that is so prevalent? Where are the fathers who take time to teach their children the way they should go? Where are the fathers who are available to hear the cries, complaints and worries of their children? The truth is, today, children enjoy their rights – to education, good health, food - but the privileges of having a father are not got. For many a home there will be no difference if the children were transferred to some well-equipped and well financed children's home. For there too, they shall have their need met but will lack the care and inner strength that is built as a result of true parental care.

The point I want to make is this; the believer does not just have a Father who is there to meet our physical needs, but One who longs and yearns to take time and show us His unfailing, unbounded and everlasting love, a Father who cares and runs after us and offers us the needed leadership and guidance every child needs. A Father who never hesitates, when need be, to discipline, rebuke and correct. A Father who's there to teach, and One who in everything sets an example for the child to follow. He is a Father who knows all and has planned the life of the child without any selfish interest in it, a Father who is willing, in a continuous and increasing way, to reveal Himself to the child. We dedicate the next couple of chapters to the privileges every child of God has.

A Loving Father

God's family is such a large one yet He loves every one of His children in a unique personal way. His love is never based on what we are or on what we do, but on who we are–children of God. That's why His love is unchanging and always available without limit to all of His children. The very fact that we, who once were lost, blind, separated from God and heading for destruction, are now called children of God is an expression of such abundant love.

> *"How great is the love the Father has lavished on us, that we should be called children of God!"* (1 John 3:1a)

The fact that you're called a child of God, you who once were an enemy, hostile towards God, in total rebellion to His interest and purpose, is an expression of God's great love. Truly when we sit and think of what we were and what we now are, all what one would honestly say is *"How great is the love the Father has lavished on us"*. Is it not a wonderful privilege to know that you have a Father who loves you for who you are; one who accepts you as you are; one always willing to pour out His love in increasing measure? You have a Father who does not just love but who by His very nature is love. The Bible says *"God is Love"* and since God is infinite and unchanging and unfading, so His love is infinite and unfading and unchanging.

The Love that Saved You—The Greatest Love

> *"Greater love has no one than this, that he lay down his life for his friends. You are my friends if you do what I command"* (John 15:13).

There's no greater love that exist than the love of Jesus that caused Him to abandon His rainbow circled Throne – His throne of glory, taking on the form of man and dying for us, laying down His life for you and me. His death was not prestigious at all, it was a shameful death, (death on a cross). Can you think of any greater love? Search for all eternity and you'll find none. It is love so amazing but true, love so ineffable. No matter how much we try to describe that love, words shall always fall short of painting a true picture of it. Frankly, the magnitude of that love can only be conceived by the Holy Spirit of God impressing it on our hearts. Even then, we shall know only in part.

The full extent of this love will only in be known in eternity. It is this love that came running after you right into the valley of sin and shame, breaking the chains which kept you bound, washed away your filth and lifted you out unto the mountain of God's glory. It is this love which caused Him to endure such an unjust and brutal treatment from the hands of sinful man, love that caused Him to endure the scorn and the shame; it is this love that caused Him to endure the pain and agony of the cross, love that caused Him who knew no sin to become sin for us, to the extent of being forsaken on the cross by the Father.

Do you remember the scene on that dark night in Gethsemane?

> *"And being in anguish, he prayed more earnestly, and his sweat was like drops of blood falling to the ground"* (Luke 22:44).

The horror of coming in contact with the sins of mankind caused Him anguish. There was no other way He could save us from the just judgment of the Father, but to carry on His body our sins. For *"He himself bore our sins in his body on the tree, so that we might die to sins and live for righteousness; by his wounds you have been healed"* (1 Peter 2:24).

He did not carry our sins only but our infirmities and grieves: *"Surely he took up our infirmities and carried our sorrows, yet we considered him stricken by God, smitten by him, and afflicted. But he was pierced for our transgressions; he was crushed for our iniquities; the punishment that brought us peace was upon him, and by his wounds we are healed"* (Isaiah 53:4-5).

Do you think that was a prestigious thing to do? That He who new such intimacy with the Father should be *"cut off from the land of the living"*? That the immortal Son of God should be *"assigned a grave with the wicked"*? That the Almighty God the Son should be *"oppressed and afflicted"* by man? The Bible says of Him: *"His appearance was so disfigured beyond that of any man and His form marred beyond human likeness"*. That's the extent to which this love that saved you went.

I recommend that you find time and read prayerfully Isaiah 52:13–Isaiah 53:12, and allow the Spirit of God to give you a glimpse of the love that saved you and the cost of your salvation. Have you seen someone who takes lightly his salvation? Then you have seen someone who has never had the slightest pinch of how much it cost God, how much it took Christ Jesus to purchase his salvation on the cross of Calvary, not mentioning the sorrows, rejection, pain and persecution He endured in the course of His ministry.

My brother, my sister, it cost God everything to wipe away your sins and give you a new life, and it has cost you nothing but your sins. And no matter what price you may have to pay to keep yourself from sin, it is yet far too negligent. It is for this reason that I believe the writer of Hebrews could ask *"How shall we escape if we ignore such a great salvation?"* (Hebrews 2:3) and that *"If we deliberately keep on sinning after we have received the knowledge of the truth, no sacrifice for sins is left, but only a fearful expectation of judgment and of raging fire that will consume the enemies of God. Anyone who rejected the law of Moses died without mercy on the testimony of two or three witnesses. How much more severely do you think a man deserves to be punished who has trampled the Son of God under foot, who has treated as an unholy thing the blood of the covenant that sanctified him, and who has insulted the Spirit of grace? For we know him who said, 'It is mine to avenge; I will repay,' and again, 'The Lord will judge his people.' 31 It is a dreadful thing to fall into the hands of the living God"* (Hebrews 10:26-31).

So please, guard your salvation with utter care, in fact with fear and trembling. Do not be ignorant of the wiles and devices of the enemy of your soul. You might have, if need be, to lay down your life in order to resist the devil and evil but take heart, God is there with you.

Love Demonstrated

"Better is open rebuke than hidden love" (Proverbs 27:5).

If God had all this love for us and hid it in His heart, without revealing it to us, it would have been meaningless. He did not just reveal this love in His word but went ahead to demonstrate this love. He says there in Proverbs that an open rebuke is preferable to hidden love. In other words, love not expressed or demonstrated is useless love. Such love will bear no fruit and will have no effect on the beloved. The God who says, *"Dear children, let us not love with words or tongue but with actions and in truth"* (1 John 3:18) has not failed to put His love in action. His is true love, without secret motives or any selfish gain or interest behind it. It is not that kind of love which pretends to offer yet to a greater extent, secretly seeks to extract.

How has God demonstrated His love for us? Principally in one way! Actually we shall try to separate it though it can still be represented as one.

The first demonstration is in the following verse:

"For God so loved the world that he gave his one and only Son, that whoever believes in him shall not perish but have eternal life" (John 3:16).

> "This is how God showed his love among us: He sent his one and only Son into the world that we might live through him" (1 John 4:9).

From these verses we can draw out the following

1. His love caused Him to give
2. His love causes us to live
3. His love has made us worthy of eternal life.
4. His love caused Him to die (Romans 5:6).

Imagine that Jesus just left His throne, took up the human form, came to earth, lived, healed and delivered people, without dying on the cross; that would have been a demonstration of God's love. He could have come and given us just a better life on earth, without life in eternity, that too would have been a demonstration of God's love. Still, He would have saved us, given us eternal life, without giving us His Son, that too would still have been a demonstration of God's love.

You see, God having given us His Son does not end in the fact that He died on the cross. It includes the fact that He is available to us, everyday, everywhere. Because God gave, we can make Jesus our possession, we can get hold of Him. In the Old Testament, only the Father was available, and the Spirit to a few chosen ones but today the Father has made the Son available to everyone who calls upon His Name. That is the demonstration of love.

Love that Endures

God's love did not end when He demonstrated it on the cross by dying for us. His love did not end when He endured all He had to both during His early life and when He went to Golgotha, but His love continues to be demonstrated even today in diverse ways. One of the ways in which God continues to demonstrate His love for you is His capacity to bear with your failures, your weaknesses and other shortcomings. God's love is what still holds back His judgment on this world of filth and rebellion. His love causes Him to yearn for the salvation of all mankind demonstrated in the exercise of His patience.

> *"The Lord is not slow in keeping his promise, as some understand slowness. He is patient with you, not wanting anyone to perish, but everyone to come to repentance"* (2 Peter 3:9).

God does not want anyone to perish, He still longs for the salvation of those who are turning their backs on Him, He longs for those who are rejecting His love outright. As long as His mercy still prevails, as long as mercy continues to stand on the way of justice, God yearns to see all come to repentance, from the most religious to the vilest of sinners.

For you His child, God's love sends Him running each time you fail, each time you fall, to lift you up and help you move on. His love causes Him to show you compassion in your shortcomings and meet your need for forgiveness. God never says, you have two last chances, after this I'll become impatient with you. He never says I've had enough from this individual. In your worst of states, His love still runs after you.

Have you sinned and felt kept aside by God? Do you feel rejected and abandoned by God because of your continuous rebellion? His forgiveness is there if you shall ask for it. For He says: *"For a brief moment I abandoned you, but with deep compassion I will bring you back. In a surge of anger I hid my face from you for a moment, but with everlasting kindness I will have compassion on you, says the LORD your Redeemer"* (Isaiah 54:7-8).

The brief moment of abandonment, is so that you can see your sin and acknowledge your guilt and ask for forgiveness. He is ready to bring you back, not just with compassion but with deep compassion. Why will God always bring you back, even when you're cast off? It is because of His unfailing love. In His love He cast you off so a godly sorrow can be borne in your heart, and this godly sorrow will lead you to repentance and repentance will lead to restoration. If only for our failures and disappointments, if only for our sins, we should have been consumed by His wrath but:

> "Because of the LORD's great love we are not consumed, for his compassions never fail. They are new every morning; great is your faithfulness" (Lamentations 3:22-23).

And though He may sometimes allow you to suffer, so you can learn some practical lessons, He will come again and again and again with His ever present compassion.

> *"For men are not cast off by the Lord forever. Though he brings grief, he will show compassion, so great is his unfailing love"* (Lamentations 3:31-32).

That is the magnitude and extent to which God's love causes Him to endure and bear. His endurance has no limits. Remember what Paul said?

> *"Love is patient… it keeps no records of wrongs … it always perseveres."*

Love Inseparable

Actually, God's love is a permanent love, no matter what we are, irrespective of color, of race, tribe etc God's love for each of His children remains permanent. Do you know that until lately, I had always thought that my sins could separate me from the love of God? Each time I read the passage in Romans 8 which talks of the fact that nothing can separate us from the love of God, I always thought in my heart that I alone can separate myself from the love of God. I always thought that if I turn my back on God, then I'll go out of His love. That is not true, because if that were the case; then God won't love the sinner, God won't love the backslider.

The fact is that our sins and backsliding can separate us from God, because He is holy but never from His love. Even His justice is part of His love. When sins are judged, God is simply giving the people concerned what is due them; in fact they're receiving their wages. God is so righteous that He won't refuse to pay anyone what he has worked for or refuse to allow him reap what he has sown. So though our sins may alienate us from God and His presence, they can never separate us from His love. Thank God we shall not allow any sin to separate us from Him or His presence. Let us examine Romans 8:35-39:

> *"Who shall separate us from the love of Christ? Shall trouble or hardship or persecution or famine or nakedness or danger or sword? As it is written: 'For your sake we face death all day long; we are considered as sheep to be slaughtered.' No, in all these things we are more than conquerors through him who loved us. For I am convinced that neither death nor life, neither angels nor demons, neither the present nor the future, nor any powers, neither height nor depth, nor anything else in all creation, will be able to separate us from the love of God that is in Christ Jesus our Lord"* (Romans 8:35-39).

In fact what the Spirit is saying here through Paul is that, the fact that you may be going through trouble and hardship, the fact that you may go without food and clothing, the fact that your very life may be at stake does not mean that God no longer loves you. This does not mean that you're separated from God's love. He did not end just with circumstances. He moved on to talk of things in the invisible; angels, demons, powers. Even these too cannot separate us from His love. He goes on to talk about time; the present or the future (maybe we should include the past). These too cannot separate us from God's love. He again talks of height and depth, these too cannot separate us from the love of God.

In the book of Isaiah, He talks of His unchanging love, which cannot be affected by natural disaster or hazards.

> *"Though the mountains be shaken and the hills be removed, yet my unfailing love for you will not be shaken nor my covenant of peace be removed, says the LORD, who has compassion on you"* (Isaiah 54:10).

Do you see the extent to which we're tied to His love? Hills may be moved i.e. part of nature may disappear but His love for us won't shake an inch. Mountains, all over the world may shake and cause tremors which take away millions of lives, yet His love would not shake or change an inch. I think we have cause to stop for a moment and worship the God of love.

The Value of God's Love

Can you tell me how much a man can pay to obtain God's love? If God were to say, child, my love is running short in supply and anyone who must get it this time around must pay for it and I make you manager of the *"God's love enterprise"*. How much will you levy for a pinch of that love? Stop for a moment and think it over for about thirty seconds.

Did you arrive at any value? My brother, my sister, nothing on earth can buy God's love, no amount of diamond, gold, silver, dollar, euro, or pound sterling can pay for the smallest portion of God's love. In fact God's love is beyond any value. It is priceless! The Psalmist understood this and exclaimed *"How priceless is your unfailing love"* (Psalm 36:7a). It is so priceless that He decided to make it free of charge, so *"both high and low among men"* may obtain it and find shelter therein.

Isn't God wonderful? Isn't He generous? Even your life laid down for His service cannot compensate the least for that love, in fact that would be *"an offering far too small"*. Relax and rest in His abundant love. The boundless sea of God's love is meant for you to sail and explore and make pleasant discoveries. The only boat which can carry you into this sea of love is Christ. As long as you're in Christ you are free to sail this sea, and I assure you that for all eternity you shall not be able to discover even half of the treasures stored up in that sea. Every stage of the journey is full of so many discoveries, not any ordinary discoveries but ones that you'll be amazed and astonished at. Each discovery will take you much time to be relieved of the excitement and celebration which comes along with it. It's a wide sea of love.

Chapter 11

THE CHILD'S PRIVILEGES 2

We have a Father who hears us, anytime, anywhere, anyhow. I do not mean that we have a Father who is aware of the sounds we make – one with a good hearing capacity. I mean a Father who listens and pays careful attention not just to the things our lips proclaim but also to the silent cries and desires and longing in the chambers of our hearts. You know that no matter how much attention our earthly fathers give us, there are moments they are not available to listen. May be after a very tiring day, he comes home falls on the bed and is deeply carried away by sleep, and then you call for two hours without getting a bit of attention. We have a heavenly Father who is always available 24/7; He takes no leave or break. *"He will neither slumber nor sleep"* but will listen and pay attention.

Remember Elijah and the prophets of Baal? Take time to go through the interesting scene in I Kings 18. It more than portrays the foolishness of those who worship idols. After having called on their god and shouted for hours without any response, listen to what Elijah told them:

> *"At noon Elijah began to taunt them: 'Shout louder!' he said, 'Surely he is a god! Perhaps he is deep in thought, or busy, or traveling. Maybe he is sleeping and must be awakened.' So they shouted louder and slashed themselves with swords and spears, as was their custom, until their blood flowed. Midday*

passed, and they continued their frantic prophesying until the time for the evening sacrifice. But there was no response, no one answered, no one paid attention" (1 Kings 18:27-29).

Their god was probably indeed too deep in thought so he couldn't hear, or maybe he was too busy so he couldn't leave what he was doing to attend to them. Haven't you seen fathers who are too busy to pay any attention to what their children have to say? Or maybe their god was traveling, hence was not available to respond to their call – Haven't you seen fathers who are always travelling such that their children have no opportunity to be attended to? Or again, maybe their god was in a deep sleep, and though they shouted louder he couldn't hear.

Are you a father who is always either in a deep thought or too busy, or always traveling such that though your children make requests or call, no matter how loud their cry, they neither receive your response, nor answer, nor attention?

Are you a Baal of a father, who allows children to call and even despair of attention, yet would not have it? You may claim to be busy doing *"the Lord's work"*: have you allowed your children to pierce their souls and slash themselves with the swords and spears of sin because you were not available on time? What account will you give to God, for the destruction of such innocent souls? I ask these questions with reverence as the Spirit lays them on my heart, for I'm not yet a father, and maybe some reading this book, may be my fathers.

The truth is that for a good percentage of church leaders, their children are a total opposite of the gospel they preach and the life they apparently live. This leads me to fear for my dear soul if that's what fatherhood is all about. God have mercy. Do you pay attention to the cries and pleas of your children? Do you pay attention to their complaints? Are there times of dialogue with your children, each one of them? Are you even available to listen? God wants you to be His model and not a model of Baal.

Unlike the scene Baal and his prophets created, God was swift to respond to the call of Elijah. Speaking of His children, He says, *"Before they call I will answer; while they are still speaking I will hear"* (Isaiah 65:24).

Do you hear that? Even before your lips pronounce the call, while it is still in your heart, God answers, no matter where you are and what time it is. While you are still speaking, trying to explain things in order to present them with reverence and honor, God says He will hear i.e. He will listen and pay attention. It is a promise, with no condition of time or location attached to it. God will hear, God will answer. He does not just wait for your call, when you feel like, He Himself is inviting you to call to Him, He longs to show you things, He longs to teach you.

Listen to His invitation: *"Call to me and I will answer you and tell you great and unsearchable things you do not know"* (Jeremiah 33:3). He invites you to call to Him, again no matter the time, no matter the place, and He will answer you. No call of yours will go unanswered by Him. Has He not promised? Will He not fulfill it? For *"God is not a man, that he should lie, nor a son of man, that he should change his mind. Does he speak and then not act? Does he promise and not fulfill?"* (Numbers 23:19)

He promises to go beyond answering what you ask, to telling you *"great and unsearchable things you do not know"*. Not just ordinary things you do not know, not any kind of cheap knowledge, but things great and unsearchable. In order words, God intends to tell you things which no matter how much you search, on your own you shall never know; things about yourself, things about your life and vocation, things about God Himself: things too great for any human mind to conceive or discover, things above the sphere of human wisdom and knowledge. That's the kind of attention our heavenly Father pays us, free access anywhere anytime, free, great and unsearchable knowledge.

"This is the confidence we have in approaching God: that if we ask anything according to his will, he hears us. And if we know that he hears us--whatever we ask--we know that we have what we asked of him" (1 John 5:14-15). This should be the confidence you and I have, even the confidence of asking and approaching, that we have a Father who hears us, who will not shun us when we approach

Him for anything and that whatever we ask, we receive. Really, there is no greater confidence we could have than this, that no request will ever be an emergency to our Father.

Maybe in the past, you hesitated asking the Father for something; maybe you thought certain things don't merit His attention. Henceforth, always call, always make your request. He listens even to your cry, when you feel like crying; cry out to Him, He won't mock you for crying over a small issue. Finally, He longs to hear your words expressing trust and confidence in Him. He longs to hear you pause moments of your day with *"I love you"* phrases that flow from your heart to Him.

A Concerned Father

Another privilege you have as a child of God is that you have a Father who is concerned about your life – present and future, One who is concerned about what happens to you every moment. He feels what you feel, and does want to be a part of your daily life. He longs that you enter into your full inheritance in Him. He longs to make you the man or woman He created you to be. There're two major ways in which God shows His concern for you: through leadership and guidance, and through Discipline. Just listen to the extent of His concern:

> *"Can a mother forget the baby at her breast and have no compassion on the child she has borne? Though she may forget, I will not forget you! See, I have engraved you on the palms of my hands; your walls are ever before me"* (Isaiah 49:15-16).

He is concerned about you, He will never forget you, you are engraved on the palms of His hand, day and night He sees you, He watches over you. He is conscious of all that happens to you.

His Leadership and Guidance

> *"In your unfailing love you will lead the people you have redeemed. In your strength you will guide them to your holy dwelling"* (Exodus 15:13).

Who are the redeemed of the Lord? Those He has saved from sin and the world. The redeemed of the Lord are God's children, redeemed by water and the blood that was shed on Calvary. God's leadership is an expression of His love and is done in His love. He will guide you in His strength to His holy dwelling. Thus, we see that God leads and guides His children in His unfailing love and strength. Such leadership and guidance is yours. The question might be asked, why does He leads and guides us? Why not leave us to ourselves?

The thing is that we live in a generation where children want to be their own masters. Some take offense at their parents who labor to lead and guide them, only to realize the guidance they so despised is what was needed to keep them from error. But it is often too late for the lesson to be learned; hearts are broken, lives destroyed, money wasted. And few have the opportunity to return home wholly like the prodigal son did.

Are you a child? Do you despise the leadership of your parents? Do you shun their guidance? Then unless you repent, nothing awaits you but self-destruction. Maybe apparently you are succeeding but I can assure you that, unless you repent and begin taking counsel and leadership from them, your fall from a staircase of success will be a great one. No one has ever violated spiritual principles and really succeeded. Your apparent success and accomplishments is just preparing you for a greater failure.

As long as parental instruction does not contradict scripture or God's clearly revealed will, the Word of God counsels and commands obedience to parents, even when they appear to be wrong. Parental authority is God's number one representative on earth and if you despise it, you despise the authority of God and you are courting not God's approval but His judgment.

1. Do you make life difficult for your parents?
2. Do you make them see you as a curse to the home rather than a blessing?
3. Do you take time to listen and pay attention to their counsel and leadership?

Again, may I say it even firmer; unless you repent, time will catch up with your rebellion to parental leadership and guidance and it will be too late to reverse the situation! God may forgive you but once the damage is caused, you shall bear the scars all your life.

God will not allow us to lead our lives the way we want because often, we are short-sighted and what appears as an egg to us may turn out to be a scorpion. May I also say that, parents who allow their children to go their own way are doing them a lot of harm, and God will call you to account? My brother, my sister, *"Hold on to instruction, do not let it go; guard it well, for it is your life"* (Proverbs 4:13) If not, *"Stern discipline awaits him who leaves the path; he who hates correction will die"* (Proverbs 15:10).

Let us return to the question as to why God should lead us. The response is simple and true.

> *"This is what the LORD says–your Redeemer, the Holy One of Israel: "I am the LORD your God, who teaches you what is best for you, who directs you in the way you should go"* (Isaiah 48:17).

He knows what is best for us, He desires to teach us these things. He directs you in the way you <u>should</u> go not in the way you feel like going or the way you want or wish to go. As the shepherd leads his sheep into green pastures and safe ground, so our Savor leads us, if we follow. Remember He is the Good Shepherd and *"He calls His own sheep by name and leads them out"*. Do not hesitate to seek His leadership and guidance. He has promised to guide you always, the Bible says so, and that is the truth; *"The Lord will guide you always"* (Isaiah 58:11a) and what is the effect of that continues and permanent guidance?

> *"He will satisfy your needs in a sun-scorched land and will strengthen your frame. You will be like a well-watered garden, like a spring whose waters never fail. Your people will rebuild the ancient ruins and will raise up the age-old foundations; you will be called Repairer of Broken Walls, Restorer of Streets with Dwellings. If you keep your feet from breaking the Sabbath and*

from doing as you please on my holy day, if you call the Sabbath a delight and the LORD's holy day honorable, and if you honor it by not going your own way and not doing as you please or speaking idle words, then you will find your joy in the LORD, and I will cause you to ride on the heights of the land and to feast on the inheritance of your father Jacob." The mouth of the LORD has spoken" (Isaiah 58:11b-14).

- He will satisfy all your needs. In other words as He guides you always, every single need of yours will be met, even when there is lack all around and when all around seems unproductive (a sun-scorched land).

- He will strengthen you. Continuous guidance is a source of strength to those who receive it. It will be a source of spiritual, mental and physical strength.

- You will be like a well-watered garden. Have you ever seen a well-watered garden? The leaves are fresh, there is manure, the flowers blossom and it appeals to everyone who passes by. More than that, it is fruitful and productive and satisfies the heart and needs of the gardener. In the same way, you will be rich spiritually and even financially, you'll bear fruits that will satisfy the heart of God and you shall meet His needs and your Christian life will be appealing to those around you, for there will be a spiritual blossom in your life.

- You will be like a spring whose waters never fail. Such a spring is reliable and continuously meets the needs of those who depend on it. You see, someone who's guided always, is one on whom people can depend, He will be a channel through which people are blessed, a channel of inspiration to those around, and a source of encouragement. Above all, it makes you a reliable person.

Guidance into Truth

> *"But when he, the Spirit of truth, comes, he will guide you into all truth. He will not speak on his own; he will speak only what he hears, and he will tell you what is yet to come"* (John 16:13).

Through the Holy Spirit, your Father seeks to guide you into the bounty of His truth. If each child of God submits to His guidance, there will be no heresy nor the numerous religious groups who today are in error because of some misinterpretation and misunderstanding of the scripture. It saves you from trouble when you are guided by the Spirit of truth. God's truth is so wide that only the Spirit of truth and can take you through a successful sail without any heretic interpretation. Trust the Spirit to guide you, express your dependence on Him. In case of doubt validate the guidance with God's written Word.

Guidance into Wisdom

> *"I guide you in the way of wisdom and lead you along straight paths. When you walk, your steps will not be hampered; when you run, you will not stumble"* (Proverbs 4:11-12).

Each one of us needs wisdom in our daily activities: at school, at home, at the job side, in church and everywhere. There are many things which God has given you the right to choose for yourself, but since godly things are discerned using godly wisdom, it will be wise to allow God to *"guide you in the way of wisdom"*: wisdom to make the right choices, wisdom to take the right decisions, wisdom to invest rightly etc. Such wisdom is always available to those who acknowledge their lack of wisdom and ask God for it. He has stated that *"If any of you lacks wisdom, he should ask God, who gives generously to all without finding fault, and it will be given to him"* (James 1:5).

The effect of God's guidance into wisdom and His leadership is that:

- When you walk your steps will not be hampered. You will easily make progress in your path and nothing will prevent you from achieving your desired end.
- When you run, you will not stumble. There're countless testimonies of businessmen who haven't made any loss whatsoever in the business because they've always depended on guidance in the way of wisdom. Much loss and pain can be avoided, as well as unnecessary wounds and bruises, if we depend on God for His wisdom. The Bible does not fail to give us the qualities of God's wisdom.

In the way of God's wisdom (see James 3), you shall walk in purity; God will guide you in the things that won't bring any impurity in your life. In the way of wisdom, you shall be peace-loving, led in the way of submissiveness. If you find *"wisdom"* leading you into rebellion against authority, then be sure that such wisdom is not from God. God's wisdom is submissive. In the way of wisdom God will lead you to exercise mercy on those who need mercy. It will lead you not just to bear fruits but good fruits in whatever you do. It will lead you to make impartial observations and judgments and reports where necessary. Finally, it brings forth sincerity in you. God's wisdom is never insincere. Even when it is to your own disadvantage, God's wisdom will always leads you to be true, honest and sincere.

For an extensive study on God's guidance and leadership, see the book *"Let God guide you Daily"* by Dr. Wesley L. Deuwel.

CHAPTER 12

THE CHILD'S PRIVILEGE 3

A Father Who Disciplines

Our Father is so responsible as to discipline us every time there is need. The Hebrew word for discipline is *mûsār*, which comes from the verb *yāsar*, which can also be translated as chasten, admonish and correct. The Greek word for discipline is *paideia*, referring to child-training and the formation of manhood. Thus from this we see that discipline is a training and correction meant to bring us to maturity (manhood).

The Reason of Discipline

God has reasons for everything He does. At times, these reasons are revealed and other times, they're not. We shall only know some of the reasons when we meet with Him in eternity. Likewise the purpose of everything He does. However, He has not failed to reveal to us some of the reasons why He disciplines us. Together let us examine some.

1. **Discipline Is Evidence of Our Legitimacy as Sons**

    "*Endure hardship as discipline; God is treating you as sons. For what son is not disciplined by his father? If you are not disciplined (and everyone undergoes discipline), then you are illegitimate children and not true sons"* (Hebrews 12:7-8).

Some people are bitter towards their parents today because they believe their parents failed to give them the discipline they needed when they were younger. God is committed to discipline us so that you and I won't be spoilt children. He disciplines you so that you will know that you're His child and therefore He has to exercise His Fatherly responsibility. No responsible father will see his child consistently going the wrong way and not exercise discipline, for this will be a passive commitment to see the child destroyed. Embrace discipline as validation of your legitimacy.

2. Discipline Is Evidence of God's Love

"…because the LORD disciplines those he loves, as a father the son he delights in" (Proverbs 3:12).

"Those whom I love I rebuke and discipline. So be earnest, and repent" (Revelations 3:19).

There's no greater love a father can show his children than to discipline them. Parents who do not discipline their children will only realize later that, all through, they have been molding them into unruly individuals. The natural man is usually stubborn and such stubbornness is far from being absent even when one is born anew. Like any other thing of the old life, God is committed to strip us of our rebellious tendencies. His discipline is there to save us from error and destruction. It is for this reason that the above verses in proverbs tell us not to despise the Lords discipline. In other words do not make light God's discipline. Our Lord further reiterates this fact in His message to the church in Laodicea. Like any other gift that stems from God's love, you and I should joyfully embrace God's discipline with gratitude instead of complaining and grumbling which only calls for sterner discipline from Him.

3. Discipline Is a Blessing

> *"Blessed is the man you discipline, O LORD, the man you teach from your law; you grant him relief from days of trouble, till a pit is dug for the wicked"* (Psalm 94:12-13).

> *"Blessed is the man whom God corrects; so do not despise the discipline of the Almighty"* (Job 5:17).

Did you ever know that God's discipline is a blessing to you? Imagine what you'll become in a few hours if God leaves you to do things the way you want. I believe, if that should happen, you'll only return at the end of the day with unfathomable disappointments, wounds and a broken heart. Maybe for now you can't really conceive how discipline can ever be a blessing, but you will when you begin to reap its fruits. Do you remember what the Bible says? *"No discipline seems pleasant at the time but painful"* but that *"later on it yields a harvest…"* Lets together, see why discipline is a blessing.

The Purpose of Discipline

Discipline like any other blessing has a purpose for which it is given–our conformity to Christ's person and character:

Firstly, God disciplines us so that we can share in His holiness.

> *"Our fathers disciplined us for a little while as they thought best; but God disciplines us for our good, that we may share in his holiness"* (Hebrews 12:10).

As earlier mentioned, God's discipline strips us of those tendencies and traits which we carry from our old life into the life to which God has called us. Since God called us to be holy, one of the ways of producing in us holiness is by disciplining us. Without this discipline you and I won't ever conform to the person and character of our Lord and Savior. *"Without holiness, no one will see the Lord"*. That's why in His love, God will spare nothing to see that you share in His holiness. Remember, we can never have any holiness of our own but can only share in God's holiness. What do you think God gains out of this? Of course nothing! *"God disciplines us for our good."* It is not for the good of your pastor, or disciple-maker or father or child or spouse but for your own very good.

Secondly, God disciplines us so we can reap a harvest of righteousness and peace.

> *"No discipline seems pleasant at the time, but painful. Later on, however, it produces a harvest of righteousness and peace for those who have been trained by it"* (Hebrews 12:11).

Righteousness here signifies being in a right relationship with God. Thus God disciplines us, so that we can reap the benefits or fruits of being in such a relationship with Him. One of the benefits or fruits of our relationship with God is that it leads us to reap the harvest of peace, peace with God, peace with man, and peace with ourselves.

Thirdly, God disciplines us so we can get a bit more serious and sincere.

> *"Those whom I love I rebuke and discipline. So be earnest, and repent"* (Revelation 3:19).

Our focus here is the word *"earnest"*. In actual fact Jesus is saying *"I love you so much as to discipline you in other that you be earnest"*. A lot of Christian folks aren't in any way serious with their Christian life. There is no sense of sincerity in whatever they do as Christians. And if not for the Lord's discipline a lot more would be in the net of waywardness hence living far below their God given capacities. So, God in His love disciplines us so that we should get more serious about the things which concern our souls. If you are to conduct a research, a large of your sample will testify that, they got more serious with spiritual things when it was very evident that God was disciplining them.

Fourthly, God disciplines us to produce in us repentance.

> *"Those whom I love I rebuke and discipline. So be earnest, and repent."*

Our focus here is the word *"Repent"* Here Jesus is saying *"I love you so much that I won't allow you to continue the wrong way, so I discipline you in order that you get a bit more serious and sincere so you can repent"*.

Have you realized that in periods when the Lord is disciplining you, you tend to be more repentant? You tend to see sin for what it really is and there is therefore that conscious *"profound change of mind involving the changing of direction of life from that of self-centeredness or sin-centeredness to God-or Christ-centeredness."* [The New International dictionary of the Bible, I.D. Douglas and Merrill C. Tenny. 1987 Zondervan]

As God disciplines you, you'll begin to get more involved in the things of God and His kingdom.

The fifth purpose for which God disciplines us is so that we will not be condemned.

> *"When we are judged by the Lord, we are being disciplined so that we will not be condemned with the world"* (1 Corinthians 11:32).

If God were not to discipline us in this life, almost all of us will live in presumption just to find on the Day of Judgment that like the world, we too lived in rebellion against God, in indifference to the things and purposes of God and in the pursuit of our own selfish interests. If not of His discipline most of us will arrive on that day just to hear Him say *"sorry I never knew you"*. Thus He disciplines us so that we won't have any accumulated charges against us. Therefore, God disciplines us to free us from condemnation. It is for this reason that Peter said, "For it is time for judgment to begin with the family of God" (I Peter 4:17a).

Methods of Discipline

1. Through trails (hardships)
2. Through persecution (opposition from men)
3. Through sufferings

4. Through periods of lack

God chooses the method(s) of discipline according to His timing and according to our need. Whatever the method employed, the ultimate purpose of His discipline is that, each one of us will increasingly become, in every way, conformed to Christ in person and in character.

CHAPTER 13

THE CHILD'S PRIVILEGES 4

A Father Who Knows All

It is such a wonderful privilege to have a Father who knows all. He is the God of all wisdom and knowledge and One who does not use His omniscience for any selfish reason but for the good of the world and especially His children. He takes no advantage over us as a result of His omniscience but seeks to use it in all respect for the good of all who name the Name of His dear Son. Praise Him!

He Knows Your Needs

> *"Do not be like them, for your Father knows what you need before you ask him"* (Matthew 6:8).

Your Father knows your needs; He knows your spiritual needs, emotional needs, material needs, and financial needs. He knows your need of protection, guidance, and direction. He is aware of the things you need which you are not even aware of. He says because you have a Father who knows all that you need, do not fret, do not let anxiety come into your heart when you feel a need. He says before you ask, He knows your need. So this should give you assurance that as you present your request He'll respond. He gives you the responsibility to tell Him of your needs and of being specific in praying for them. He knows even your most silent need of love, comfort and encouragement and is always ready to provide if you in humility make your requests known to Him.

Before you and I could ever be aware of our need of salvation, He made provision for it, and worked things out on our behalf, so we could be recipients of this great favor. In the same way, He knows the needs of the sinner, He sees their need for mercy, compassion and forgiveness and He longs to meet them.

Have you realized that when you've sinned and are unconscious of your need for His pardon, He woos you, shows you your need of forgiveness and restoration? Even those sins which are long forgotten or buried in the darkest corner of our hearts, He sheds His light in there and says "Hey son, you need forgiveness for this stuff in here, send it out and receive my pardon". What joy floods our souls during such times, what peace fills our heart during such times! Glory to His Name!

He Knows Your Weakness

> *"For he knows how we are formed, he remembers that we are dust"*
> (Psalm 103:14).

Our Father is our creator, He knows both our strengths and our weaknesses, so when you manifest such weaknesses, they are never a surprise to Him. He never gets mad at you when you fall or fail. He knows that you were made from dust, so He understands the weaknesses of your flesh. Such knowledge of your weaknesses causes Him to allow no temptation which you can't bear to come your way. He understands your threshold capacity in every domain and won't allow anything which will destroy you. He knows and understands your character weaknesses and seeks to replace them with His strength. Remember what Paul said:

> *"But he said to me, 'My grace is sufficient for you, for my power is made perfect in weakness.' Therefore I will boast all the more gladly about my weaknesses, so that Christ's power may rest on me. That is why, for Christ's sake, I de-*

light in weaknesses, in insults, in hardships, in persecutions, in difficulties. For when I am weak, then I am strong" (2 Corinthians 12:9-10).

Do not condemn yourself for the weaknesses you manifest, glory in them and seek Christ's power to live above your weakness. Use them as an opportunity to draw nearer to God and to depend on Him. Remember that you *"can do all things through Christ who strengthens"* you. Even in areas where you think you are strong, do not rely an inch on your strength. But trust God for His own strength. The hymn writer says, *"The arm of flesh shall fail you; ye dare not trust your own"*. Do not count even on your will and determination, only God knows what lies ahead and He alone can better prepare you for the future.

He Knows Your Thoughts (Mind)

> *"The LORD knows the thoughts of man; he knows that they are futile"*
> (Psalm 94:11).

Have you ever tried to hide something from the Lord? I have, but I came to realize how foolish I was. Yet there are many who think God does not know their thoughts and they shun God's *"immediate presence"* in an attempt to hide from Him. My brother, my sister, God knows each thought that passes through your mind, the secret meditations and imaginations and motives of your mind. He knows them all. This shouldn't frighten you, it should make you all the more confident, even to ask Him to show you your mind, the end of which is that you shall be cleansed if there was any sin within your mind.

He Knows Your Heart

> *"...would not God have discovered it, since he knows the secrets of the heart?"*
> (Psalm 44:21)

God knows the secrets of your heart, the kind of things you desire. He knows the things that occupy your heart. He knows when your actions conform to the desires of your heart. He knows the secrets of your heart, your secret plans and scheming, your secret hopes. He knows how deceitful the heart of man is.

> *"The heart is deceitful above all things and beyond cure. Who can understand it?"* (Jeremiah 17:9)

In fact, He knows it is beyond cure. No one can understand the degree of corruptness of the heart of man but God, that's why at conversion, God took away your old heart (heart of stone) and gave you a new heart (heart of flesh). This was His promise to you as an unbeliever.

> *"I will give you a new heart and put a new spirit in you; I will remove from you your heart of stone and give you a heart of flesh"* (Ezekiel 36:26).

When you turned to Him, He did fulfill this promise by giving you a new and undivided heart. You have the responsibility to guard this new heart and keep it pure and undivided. Do you notice how undivided and committed young converts are? It is because their new heart is still pure and kept from contamination. As years pass by, as you allow things to come into your heart; it becomes polluted and once again divided and here God gives you the responsibility to purge your heart of all impurities (sins and idols). Examine the nature of your heart in light of the following conditions revealed in scripture:

1. Heart of stone or heart of flesh *(Ezekiel 36:26)*
2. Undivided or divided heart *(Ezekiel 14:19)*
3. Pure or impure heart *(Matthew 5:8, Ps 51:10)*
4. A broken or unbroken heart *(Psalm 51:17)*
5. A free or bound heart *(Psalm 119:32)*
6. A sick or healthy heart *(Proverbs 13:12)*
7. A wise or foolish heart *(Ecclesiastes 8:5)*
8. A cheerful or gloomy heart *(Proverbs 17:22)*
9. A Committed or uncommitted heart *(I Kings 8:61)*
10. A hardened and unyielding heart *(Exodus 8:32, 9:7)*

As you read each of the passages, you'll notice the characteristics of heart condition, and ask God to show you your heart in the light of those characteristics.

He Knows Those Who Are His

One evening I went with my friend Rick to the internet to check mails and a fun page had been sent to him by an e-pal, so he invited me to share in the fun. One of the stories on the fun page went thus (please I'll not be able to narrate it word for word, but would try as much as possible to keep in line);

> *"There was a young lady whose husband was desperate to have a son but her two first pregnancies brought forth two beautiful daughters. When she got pregnant the third time, the husband threatened to file in a divorce if it were not a baby boy this time around. Fortunately the wife put to bed a baby boy; only he looked like a monster, ugly and quite contrary in beauty to the girls. The man was disappointed and said to the wife 'Honey, I can't understand why our two girls are so beautiful and this boy comes out so ugly. Did you cheat on me this time around?' The wife responded 'No! Darling I was very faithful at least I didn't cheat on you this time around.'"*

Do you see the fun in it? All this time the guy had thought he had two beautiful daughters and so was probably proud of another man's children but was quick to reject his own son, because he thought he could not give birth to such an ugly fellow, only for him to know the shocking truth later. You see, a lot of folks out there are deceived to assume responsibilities over children who are not theirs. Worst still, there're so many children out there who hardly know their illegitimate parents. This reminds me of a friend's grandfather whose son (whom he didn't know) came looking for him. A son who himself was already a man of about 50. The only thing that could convince the grand Pa that it is his son was their resemblance.

Though men may try to conduct all forms of test to prove whether a child is theirs or not, God does not need to carry out any DNA test or any of its sort, to prove the legitimacy of His children. A lot of supposed Christian folks out there are just playing games with God. In fact they think they can play games with God in trying to pretend that they are believers. They go to church, take part in Christian activities and even appear to pray and receive answers but have never made Jesus their Lord and Savior, they have never experienced the saving and transforming power of the Savior and have continued in their normal life of sin and rebellion. If you are playing games with God, you better stop the game and get saved. Being always in the midst of God's children doesn't make you one. For *"Nevertheless, God's solid foundation stands firm, sealed with this inscription: 'The Lord knows those who are his,' and, 'Everyone who confesses the name of the Lord must turn away from wickedness'"* (2 Timothy 2:19).

You see, those who are God's must turn away from wickedness. If there's any sin you practice, you had better turn away from it before you receive your shock. That's God's own DNA test. It is not meant for Him but for those who are deceived into thinking they are God's children.

Hey! This reminds me of another class of people who live in the deception that they are the only legal Christians. In fact, according to them, all others Christians are illegal. Imagine the degree of their deception! The Bible says:

> *"For I can testify about them that they are zealous for God, but their zeal is not based on knowledge. Since they did not know the righteousness that comes from God and sought to establish their own, they did not submit to God's righteousness"* (Romans 10:2-3).

Many people are very zealous for God, but their zeal is not based on knowledge. Why, because they do not know the righteousness that comes from God, hence they have sought to establish their own righteousness (penances, laws, etc. forgetting to know that God's righteousness is faith in Jesus Christ, not putting on this or that in order to look pius and sanctimonious), refused justification by faith, and are preaching a justification which comes through works–what heresy. However, *"Christ is the end of the law so that there may be righteousness for everyone who believes"* (Romans 10:4).

What measureless inheritance we do have as children of God, what measureless privileges God has given each one of us as children. Up to now, all what we've done is far from being exhaustive of the inheritance and privileges of the child of God. In the next chapter, we shall see how we can use our inheritance and privileges to carry out our responsibilities as children of God. Our Father desires to see us grow into responsible people and fulfill that which He prepared for us before the foundations of the world to accomplish. This leads us to the next section *"The child's responsibilities"*. What I've tried to do is examine the basic responsibilities of every child, anywhere any time– what I term the general responsibilities of every child of God. We all know, there are 'personal' responsibilities in the Body of Christ, usually determined by our gifts, talents and ministries given us by our Father.

CHAPTER 14

THE CHILD'S RESPONSIBILITY

The Child's Responsibilty

Which child doesn't feel honored when he/she realizes the parents are given him/her responsibilities to carry? It makes you know your *"importance and self-worth"* and you feel trusted by your parents. It makes you know that you are capable of doing something and that they have confidence in you. In the same light God has given us, as children, responsibilities.

> *"And now, O Israel, what does the LORD your God ask of you but to fear the LORD your God, to walk in all his ways, to love him, to serve the LORD your God with all your heart and with all your soul, and to observe the LORD's commands and decrees that I am giving you today for your own good?"* (Deuteronomy 10:12-13).

From the above verses, we can draw out the following things which our Father asks of us.

1. To fear the Lord your God
2. To walk in His ways
3. To love Him
4. To serve Him with all your heart and with all your soul

5. To observe His commands and decrees

Love Reciprocated

> *"He answered: 'Love the Lord your God with all your heart and with all your soul and with all your strength and with all your mind'; and, 'Love your neighbor as yourself'"* (Luke 10:27).

After all God has done for you, in all He is doing and will do for you, God just expects that you love Him, that you reciprocate the love He has shown you. He longs to put His love in your own heart in increasing measures so you too can indeed love Him, with the same love He gives you. Why? Because human love is so limited and finite, selfish and unstable!

Our Father has asked us to love Him, even as He has loved us. He's not asking for a one way affair, He's the first to love us and show us His love in a million ways. All what He asks of us, all that He asks of you is *"for your own good."* Loving Him is for your own good, serving Him is for your own good, obeying Him is for your own good. He gains nothing, you gain everything.

How are you to love the Lord?

1. with all your heart
2. with all your soul
3. with all your strength
4. with all your mind

Loving the Lord with all your heart means, God is to be the only object of your love; He alone is to occupy the heart and nothing else. Your heart must be fully committed to Him with undivided devotion. Nothing should compete with Him in your heart, nothing should come before Him and nothing should be His second. When you love Him with all your heart, He directs your love to the things you must love, which He sees good for you, both in this life and in the one to come.

Loving the Lord with all your soul means

- All your will
- All your emotions
- All your mind

Must be involved in loving the Lord, none should be left aside.

You may ask *"what are the practical implications of this?"*

I believe to love the Lord your God with all your will implies having your will aligned with God's will, be willing to do that which God wants you to do and be determined in your pursuit of God. In the things of God, willingness implies determination: when you're willing you have to be determined.

Loving God involves emotions too, not in part but in whole. Your emotions are to be attached to Him. This means the things which bring God joy should bring you joy, the things which cause Him sorrow and pain, should cause you sorrow and pain.

Loving the Lord with all your mind implies allowing thoughts of Him to fill your mind, actively thinking about Him, meditating on His love, goodness and care for you. It implies you *"fix your thoughts on Jesus"* (Hebrews 3:1). To fix your thoughts on Jesus means to think about Him with great attention i.e. with great interest and care.

Loving the Lord with all your strength involves your intellectual, emotional, psychological, physical, and why not your financial strength?

There are two ways in which love for God can be readily manifested.

1. Loving His children
2. Obedience to His commands

Loving God's Children (Love Extended)

> *"Dear friends, since God so loved us, we also ought to love one another"* (1 John 4:11).

> *"And he has given us this command: Whoever loves God must also love his brother"* (1 John 4:21).

Why are you to love others?

The first reason is because God loved you. There's no other reason for you to love someone else. Not even because he/she has been good to you or loves you. The only basis of your love for anyone should be Christ's love for you. If this is so, your love for that person whoever it may be, will be unchanging, not based on merit or your abilities or anything else. It is like God is saying here, that if you want to succeed in your love for your fellowman, the only basis, the only firm foundation, the only guarantee is His love for you. All else will fail, any other foundation will crumble through the tests.

The second reason is that He commands you to love others (more on this later.)

Thirdly, you love others as a prove of your love for God, *"If anyone says, 'I love God,' yet hates his brother, he is a liar. For anyone who does not love his brother, whom he has seen, cannot love God, whom he has not seen"* (1 John 4:20).

You see, God is saying *"to prove your love for Me, show love to your brother and to those around you, even the sinner, even those who hate and persecute you."*

Practically, this means, mourning with your brother who mourns, sharing with those in need, caring for those who need prayers, blessing those who need your blessings. Remember what John says, *"This is how we know what love is: Jesus Christ laid down his life for us. And we ought to lay down our lives for our brothers. If anyone has material possessions and sees his brother in need but has no pity on him, how can the love of God be in him? Dear children, let us not love with words or tongue but with actions and in truth"* (I John 3:16-18).

It is not just a matter of thinking love in your heart but of demonstrating it by your daily actions, your daily choices and decisions.

I wrote some prayer topics from 1 Corinthians 13:4-7 and put in the prayer chain room at our student centre, when I was part of the leadership that year. I remember in one of the Friday prayer meetings (6:00 pm – 10:00 pm) as I led the brethren to pray through the topics, there was much heart searching and repentance because each of us, in one way or the other found that, true and practical love was somehow lacking. You can use them to pray for any group or your local church as a whole.

I believe the reason why many people don't really experience God's love is because they won't give out love. The reason why many children of God are not really certain about their Father's love – supreme love for them is because they won't express and put love in action for their fellow man. The greatest spiritual principle is to give when you need and you shall have what you need.

> *"Give, and it will be given to you. A good measure, pressed down, shaken together and running over, will be poured into your lap. For with the measure you use, it will be measured to you"* (Luke 6:38).

Give out your love, give out care, give out your possession and resources, then you shall have them in greater measure. It is in this light that Paul says,

> *"And I pray that you, being rooted and established in love, may have power, together with all the saints, to grasp how wide and long and high and deep is the love of Christ, and to know this love that surpasses knowledge--that you may be filled to the measure of all the fullness of God"* (Ephesians 3:17b-19).

Do you see what He says? In order to be able to know this love that surpasses knowledge, in order to be filled to the measure of all the fullness of God, in order to have power to know the depth, width, height and length of God's love, you must first be rooted and established in love.

What does He mean by being rooted in love? He simply means being strongly influenced by love. As you allow God's love to influence you, your actions, your choices, taste, your attitudes and behavior, then you'll begin to see the dimensions of God's love, experiencing it to the full.

As you pray, set out to action. S.D Gordon said *"you can do more than pray after you have prayed but you cannot do more than pray until you have prayed"*. My pastor, Roger Forteh always said *"a man has prayed when he has acted out what he prayed"*.

Look for opportunities to give out your love, not just to friends but to those you aren't close to. There's always something to give, no matter how small, if done out of love, it will greatly bless the recipient and leave a footprint in his life. So *"Be imitators of God, therefore, as dearly loved children and live a life of love, just as Christ loved us and gave himself up for us as a fragrant offering and sacrifice to God"* (Ephesians 5:1-2). As you imitate Christ in His love for mankind you will be able to lay your life or anything that is precious to you on behalf of another whose need is more than yours. We do not give because we have excess, we give to make provision for someone whose need may be more urgent that ours. Sacrificial gifts are always a fragrant offering to the Lord.

Observing God's Commands (Obedience As Love)

"This is love for God: to obey his commands. And his commands are not burdensome" (1 John 5:3).

"And this is love: that we walk in obedience to his commands" (2 John 6a).

"If you love me, you will obey what I command" (John 14:15).

Love for God is manifested in your obedience to His commands. Love cannot be separated from obedience, where one is lacking the other is lacking. You can measure your degree of love for the Lord by your promptness in obeying Him to the full as long as His instruction is made clear to you. Thus you can know your degree of love for the Lord by evaluating how much of His words you are putting into practice.

Chapter 15

The Child's Responsibility 2

The Fear of The Lord

There's no other virtue with so many implications like the fear of the Lord. Here, fear talks of reverence and awe for God. We shall include honor and respect in what we'll refer to as fear of the Lord i.e. here, each time we use the word fear, it will mean any of all of the following:

1. Reverence
2. Honor
3. Awe

God desires to be feared, He expects us, or to better put it demands that He be feared. Usually, even amongst the saved, there's the lack of the fear of the Lord. Unwholesome talk, coarse joking, gossip, slander, criticism all indicate lack of the fear of the Lord. Can God smile over this lack of fear for Him? Never! Throughout scripture, He has rebuked Priests, Prophets, as well as ordinary Israelites when He was being treated with contempt. Somewhere He asked,

> *"A son honors his father, and a servant his master. If I am a father, where is the honor due me? If I am a master, where is the respect due me?" says the*

> LORD Almighty. 'It is you, O priests, who show contempt for my name. But you ask, 'How have we shown contempt for your name?'" (Malachi 1:6)

Do you see those heart-searching questions? It is very clear that some of us treat God in a way that we won't dare treat our earthly fathers. How come we've been so deceived to think God wouldn't feel despised when treated that way? We've lived in such presumption for so long. God demands the honor due Him as a Father and the respect due Him as a Master. The worse is that, it is done by us, priests of the New Covenant. To better understand all that will be said here, please I advise you to take off 20 minutes at least, to read through the book of Malachi.

When I meditated on this verse, this is what I wrote, there, alone in God's presence:

How does a servant respect his Master?
- By carrying out the Master's commands on time.
- By being at the post of duty i.e. rendering proper service due the master.
- Being available to the master at all times
- Taking instructions from the master
- Waiting on the master.

How does a servant disrespect his master?
- Not being at the place of duty.
- Obeying his master with grumbling
- Disobeying his master
- Arguing with his master
- Questioning his master's authority
- Not being available to the master
- Carrying out the master's instruction when he (the servant) deems best
- When do I disrespect the Lord (particularly)?
- Do anything without seeking His will about it
- Show less than maximum concern for His interest and purposes
- Do anything I'll not do in the presence of a senior earthly authority.

The Child's Responsibility 2

Day 1, 40 Minutes

How does a son honor his father?
- Obey Him in all things
- Respect him at all time
- Give him the best in everything
- Do all to lift up his name (make him proud),

When does a son dishonor his father? When he:
- Disobeys him
- Grumbles against him
- Speak ill (before or behind) of him
- Responds late to his call
- Puts himself before the father
- Rubs the father's name in the mud

When do I dishonor the Lord (particularly)?
- Eat without saying grace
- Don't give Him the first fruits of my labor
- Come late to His presence
- Leave any how from His presence
- Assume any posture in His presence
- Don't present my offerings in time
- Postpone repentance
- Question His workings in me
- Doubt His love and promises
- Don't give Him the best of all I am and have
- Question His choices for me

In the whole of Malachi 1, God's major problem is that we dare to do things to Him which we can't dare to do in the presence of some earthly authority. Take for example late coming; usually in meetings presided over by say a Governor or Mayor, no one is allowed to come into the premises of the meeting when the Governor is already there. But do you see how believers stroll late into God's presence? People who probably in the last hour before the meeting were literally doing nothing important? Maybe painting up, trying to look good on the outside, to appear appealing to the eyes of men.

My brother, may I tell you today and now that late coming is a sin, whether you acknowledge it or not, God is grieved each time we keep Him waiting. I am quite sure that in meetings where one is late, unless there's deep repentance, one's name appears absent on heaven's roll call. It is a hard truth, but I believe it is real.

Another great evil even among God's people is the fact that some see God as one worthy of their leftovers. The money they have no use for is the one they offer to God. One thing is sure; all that you offer to God which is not your best is unacceptable. All that which cost you nothing is unacceptable before God, man may accept it but God will not record it as a gift made to Him or as a sacrifice pleasing to Him. God wants your all without defect. He wants the best of you, your time, your money, your strength, intellect etc. It is either the best or nothing.

Everything you do half-heartedly is a waste of time and resources. God will not compromise the honor and respect due Him. All that you won't do with joy and sense of gratitude is abominable before God, not only is it useless. Many of us, instead of resting before prayer meetings run after vain pursuits only to come after being exhausted to sleep in God's presence. May God speak to our hearts and may we respond through repentance in sackcloth and ashes.

Are you a God cheater?

> "But you profane it by saying of the Lord's table, 'It is defiled,' and of its food, 'It is contemptible.' And you say, 'What a burden!' and you sniff at it contemptuously," says the LORD Almighty. "When you bring injured, crippled or diseased animals and offer them as sacrifices, should I accept them from your hands?" says the LORD. "Cursed is the cheat who has an acceptable male in his flock and vows to give it, but then sacrifices a blemished animal to the Lord. For I am a great king," says the LORD Almighty, "and my name is to be feared among the nations" (Malachi 1:12-14).

On meditating on this passage, this is what I wrote in my meditation note book:

When do I cheat God?
- Anytime I offer to God anything less than the best I can offer
- Each time I do less than that which I've committed myself to do
- When I pray for 1 hour 55 minutes when I've committed myself to pray for 2hrs.
- When I fast for 2 days instead of 3 days I'm a cheat.
- When I give 12% when I've committed myself to give 15%

All that which I don't consider it an honor or privilege to render and thus do it with joy is abominable before God.

- If I can meditate for 45 minutes and decide to do it for 40 minutes I am a cheat
- If I can read 16 chapters of the Bible daily and I decide to read 4 chapters I am a great cheat; I am cheating God with respect to time spent in communion with Him.

NB: Most of the things above are very personal, God spoke to me according to what I was supposed to do with respect to my commitments made. Thus I am not setting any standard for others.

Is Your Heart Set to Please The Lord?

From Malachi 1:14b, we see that God is committed to see His Name feared among the nations (the heathen) but it must first begin with His children. He is committed to see His fear reign in your life, in every aspect of it.

> "And now this admonition is for you, O priests. If you do not listen, and if you do not set your heart to honor my name," says the LORD Almighty, "I will send a curse upon you, and I will curse your blessings. Yes, I have already cursed them, because you have not set your heart to honor me.

> *"Because of you I will rebuke your descendants; I will spread on your faces the offal from your festival sacrifices, and you will be carried off with it"* (Malachi 2:1-3).

The dangers of not setting one's heart to honor God are great and the consequences far reaching, it doesn't end with you but goes down to your descendants. Please even for the sake of your descendant set your heart to honor the Lord, He is worthy of it. Set your heart to please Him, it is not an easy affair, but by His grace each one of us can continue on that path.

What are the implications of setting your heart to honor the Lord?
1. A wholehearted commitment to obey the Lord.
2. A wholehearted commitment to honesty, truth and integrity.
3. A wholehearted commitment to see God glorified.
4. A wholehearted commitment to live under the influence of the Holy Spirit.
5. A wholehearted commitment to present my best and my all in everything.
6. A wholehearted commitment to holiness and righteousness.
7. A wholehearted commitment to total separation from the world.
8. A wholehearted commitment to the Will of God.
9. A wholehearted laying down of all rights on the altar of the gospel of Christ.
10. A heart completely abandoned in the hands of God.

The Fear of The Lord, What It Is

> *"Come, my children, listen to me; I will teach you the fear of the LORD. Whoever of you loves life and desires to see many good days, keep your tongue from evil and your lips from speaking lies. Turn from evil and do good; seek peace and pursue it"* (Psalm 34:11-14).

What are the practicalities of fearing the Lord?
1. Keeping your tongue from evil
2. Keeping lips from speaking lies

3. Turning from evil and doing good
4. Seeking peace and pursuing it

The tongue is such a vital part of man that no other part of the body other than the heart has received such attention in scripture. With the tongue we speak the Word of God, with the tongue we encourage one another, with it we praise our God and Father, with it we pray and preach the gospel. What usefulness has the tongue, yet the tongue can be as destructive as it is useful. With it we decide the fate of many, we can crush the spirit of others, by it we decide our fate *"for by your words you will be acquitted, and by your words you will be condemned"* (Matthew 12:37).

Can you recall what James said concerning the tongue?

> *"Likewise the tongue is a small part of the body, but it makes great boasts. Consider what a great forest is set on fire by a small spark. The tongue also is a fire, a world of evil among the parts of the body. It corrupts the whole person, sets the whole course of his life on fire, and is itself set on fire by hell. All kinds of animals, birds, reptiles and creatures of the sea are being tamed and have been tamed by man, but no man can tame the tongue. It is a restless evil, full of deadly poison"* (James 3:5-8).

In fact the tongue poses more to us than we seem to realize. Beyond everything else, it saps away spiritual power. That's why *"men will have to give account on the Day of Judgment for every careless word they have spoken"* (Matthew 12:36). The only remedy from the dangers of the tongue is the Fear of God, if allowed to control what comes out of your mouth, the kind of conversations you partake in. In fact, *"If anyone considers himself religious and yet does not keep a tight rein on his tongue, he deceives himself and his religion is worthless"* (James 1:26) and so David could desperately pray for God to set a guard over his mouth and to keep watch over the door of his lips (Psalm 14:3). What has been said for the tongue can well apply to the lips.

The fear of the Lord implies turning from evil and doing Good. In fact *"to fear the Lord is to hate evil"* (Prov. 8:13a) and what is evil? *"Pride and arrogance, evil behavior and perverse speech"* (Proverbs 8:13b). Man, there're moments you really feel led into sin and if there's no fear of God in your heart you'll give in. But what shall keep you from sin, even when sin seems to bring the greatest gain is the fear of the Lord, if you allow it to reign in your heart.

What You Need

"…give me an undivided heart, that I may fear your name" (Psalm 86:11b).

Until now, I have just talked of the fear of God which we so desperately need, in order to *"walk in white"* in this world of filth and stains of sin all round. Each one of us could acknowledge that the pressure of sin and of the world on the soul of the child of God is great, sin is increasingly growing cheap, new ways of sinning are invented, some very appealing to the sinful nature. More than ever before, sin knocks violently at the door of the heart of the child of God, hoping to be offered an opportunity of dinning and wining on the table set on the heart of God's elect. The offers are great and to resist with the head lifted up, there must be a deep fear of the Lord in the heart.

Have you seen two saints under the same condition faced with sin and one gives in while the other does not? The reason is that the fear of the Lord reigned in one heart while it didn't in the other. My, sister, my brother, there're moments when sin come running after your soul, making its offers of pleasure and gain. During such moments what you need is not to resist but flee from sin with all you might, and this energy can only be tapped from the infinite reservoir of the fear of the Lord, which will carry you on "wings like eagle's" to soar to the heights of God's holiness and righteousness.

How can you therefore fear the Lord? What is it you need? An undivided heart is what you need in order to fear God; a heart that has resolved to go the long way of righteousness and holiness; a heart which has resolved to travel the path of honoring and fearing the Lord; a heart which does not waiver between God and some other thing: gain, pleasure, fame, sex, reputation, etc; a heart which will not waiver between upholding God's glory, holiness and purity, and protection of self-image.

Only God can give you an undivided heart, like David, cry out to Him day and night and it will be yours. In fact it is a promise and you can stand on it to make your claim. He says, *"I will give them an undivided heart and put a new spirit in them; I will remove from them their heart of stone and give them a heart of flesh. Then they will follow my decrees and be careful to keep my laws. They will be my people, and I will be their God"* (Ezekiel 11:19-20). Tell Him you want to walk in white in this world of filth and stain.

The Benefits of the Fear of The Lord

We've talked about the fear of the Lord, what it is and what you need in order to fear the Lord. Together let's examine some of the benefits associated with the fear of the Lord. Remember I said from the beginning of this section that no other virtue has implications like the fear of the Lord, besides causing you to walk in white, there're many exclusive benefits for those who fear the Lord.

First, those who fear the Lord have their names written in a scroll of remembrance right in the presence of God. It is not just a scroll on which the name of every child of God is written but a special scroll in which only those executing their responsibility of fearing the Lord have their names written. It is a scroll of remembrance and God uses it to remember you always. Each time He opens the scroll, He sees your name on it (if you fear the Lord) and it pleases Him.

> *"Then those who feared the LORD talked with each other, and the LORD listened and heard. A scroll of remembrance was written in his presence concerning those who feared the LORD and honored his name"* (Malachi 3:16).

Amongst His children, only those who fear Him and honor His Name have this privilege to have their names written there. You can have yours written there too by making a commitment to fear the Lord and honor His Name in whatever circumstance. A special reward is reserved in heaven for all who fear the Lord.

In the days of Malachi God was robbed, slandered, dishonored, and despised. It was the normal trend of the day to commit sin, to speak harsh things about

God. It was considered *"futile to serve God"*. There seemed to be no gain in serving the Lord or keeping His commands. The arrogant were considered blessed, evil doers prospered and those who challenged God escaped. Is it very different from ours? Certainly not!

All across the world, governments and parliaments are rising up to challenge God by passing bills and laws which are contrary to God's law, science is rising to its climax of promoting godlessness, children of God are considered fools. But the Lord says, *"Surely the day is coming; it will burn like a furnace. All the arrogant and every evildoer will be stubble, and that day that is coming will set them on fire,"* says the LORD Almighty. *"Not a root or a branch will be left to them. But for you who revere my name, the sun of righteousness will rise with healing in its wings. And you will go out and leap like calves released from the stall"* (Malachi 4:1-2).

Second, those who fear the Lord have their protection secure as God keeps a special watch over them and over their affairs:

> *"The angel of the LORD encamps around those who fear him, and he delivers them"* (Psalm 34:7).

> *"He who fears the LORD has a secure fortress, and for his children it will be a refuge"* (Proverbs 14:26).

Do you see it? God's angel encamps round those who fear Him. He who fears the Lord has a secure fortress, not just for Him but also for his children. As you fear the Lord, you are preparing a refuge for your children. When calamity comes they'll always have a place to hide their head and besides *"the eyes of the Lord are on those who fear Him"* (Psalm 33:18a).

Third, those who fear the Lord lack nothing, they have their needs met, no matter what they apparently loss in terms of dishonest gain. Nothing means nothing, nothing is exclusive of nothing; God says you'll lack nothing if you fear Him and that is what it means. Do you want all your needs met? Then set your heart on fearing the Lord.

Fourth, the fear of the Lord brings direction. God would direct those who fear Him, who refuse to make any move without His approval.

> *"Who, then, is the man that fears the LORD? He will instruct him in the way chosen for him"* (Psalm 25:12).

He will give you instructions in the path He wants you to tread, He will give you traveling directives on how you should travel in the path He has chosen for you, He will teach you how to read signs on that path? Do not walk on a path chosen for another person.

Fifth, those who fear the Lord win His confidence.

> *"The LORD confides in those who fear him; he makes his covenant known to them"* (Psalm 25:14).

To confide means to tell somebody secrets and personal information that you do not want other people to know. Man, God has things He tells only those who fear Him, others are not privileged to know those things. Remember He told Daniel, John, and Paul some things and asked them to seal the things they had heard? (Daniel 12:4, Revelations 10:4, 2 Corinthians 12:4). Even in our age, some men are given secrets that ordinary Christians won't know because God confines in them. Have you heard people talk about covenants with God? God will not make a covenant with those who do not fear Him, for today or tomorrow, when pressure comes they will break the covenant and bring on themselves judgment.

Sixth, the fear of the Lord is a fountain of life.

> *"The fear of the LORD is a fountain of life, turning a man from the snares of death"* (Proverbs 14:27).

> *"The fear of the LORD leads to life: Then one rests content, untouched by trouble"* (Proverbs 19:23).

The fear of the Lord leads to life, those who fear the Lord will always find life. More than that, it is in itself *"a fountain of life"*. In simple words, the fear of the Lord is a rich source of life. Why? Because it turns a man from the snares of death! You see, death will not come openly. It is first an unwanted enemy who can only approach unidentified through snares. A snare is a situation which seems attractive but is unpleasant and difficult to escape from. The fear of the Lord is what causes you to escape these snares all around. It will cause you to see the hook behind every bait, the pain behind every pleasure. It will keep you from every *"way that seems right to a man but in the end leads to death"*, it will cause you to see every joy which leads to grief and laughter which leads to heart ache. Do you love life? Then let the fear of God reign in your heart.

The seventh benefit is that the fear of the Lord is a blessing. It doesn't just bring those blessings listed until now but is in itself a blessing for those who possess it.

> *"Blessed are all who fear the LORD, who walk in his ways. You will eat the fruit of your labor; blessings and prosperity will be yours. Your wife will be like a fruitful vine within your house; your sons will be like olive shoots around your table. Thus is the man blessed who fears the LORD"* (Psalm 128:1-4).

Do we need any further explanation from these verses? Your wife's productivity in every realm, your children's behavior and productivity will depend on how much you fear the Lord.

The eighth benefit is that the fear of the Lord earns a special dose of God's delight.

> *"The LORD delights in those who fear him"* (Psalm 147:11a).

To delight in someone is to have a feeling of great pleasure in that person. Thus God takes pleasure in those who fear Him. He loves them and shows them His compassion (Psalm 103:11,13).

The ninth benefit is that those who fear the Lord enjoy God's goodness.

> *"How great is your goodness, which you have stored up for those who fear you, which you bestow in the sight of men on those who take refuge in you"* (Psalm 31:19).

It is not His normal goodness He shows to all His children but a great goodness stored up especially for those who have made the fear of the Lord their possession. He has not just stored up the goodness but goes ahead to bestow the goodness on them even in the sight of men. In other words God's goodness to you will be evident to all around you.

Finally, the fear of the Lord is the beginning of wisdom. It is the start point of wisdom, the first sign of a man or a woman possessing wisdom. *"The fear of the LORD is the beginning of wisdom"* (Psalm 111:10a). In other words, the fear of the Lord opens the way to possessing wisdom.

Chapter 16

The Child's Responsibility 3

Trusting The Lord

To trust the Lord is to believe that the Lord is good, sincere, honest, caring, loving etc. and will not try to harm or deceive you. We live in a world which is not our home, in a world which is a contested territory between heaven and hell. The ruler of this world is mad at Christians and seeks ever always to destroy the Christian or to render him powerless and ineffective. Remember Peter's description of him: *"Your enemy the devil prowls around like a roaring lion looking for someone to devour"* (I Peter 5:8). He throws his fiery darts everywhere every time. In this world the Christian shall be tested, he shall suffer; painful trials shall be the lot of he who has decided to go *"full scale"* with the Lord.

There're moments when the Christian will feel forsaken and heaven will seem so silent over what is happening to you. It will be as though heaven has taken side with hell against you. Dreams will fade, castles built will collapse and God will seem to be *"so far away, a million miles or more"* with each passing day. At such moments, nothing will keep you going but trust. Believe that the Lord is good, that He seeks your good in everything, and that He works for your good in all things. Believe that He can neither deceive nor harm you and that one day even in the deepest darkness, *"the sun of righteousness will rise with healing in its wings"*. This healing brings deliverance, and comfort, and will carry you on wings to soar the heights of God's love, peace and joy that those who haven't been through *"fiery ordeals"* will never know. Dear, all you need to do is to believe the scripture that says *"And we know that in all things God works for the good of those who love Him"* (Romans 8:28). This is the secret to a victorious and happy Christian life. Are we not called *"believers"*? For that's what we really are. We believe God for His person, His character and His workings as revealed in His Word – the Holy Scriptures.

Trusting in Him

> *"But I trust in you, O LORD; I say, 'You are my God'"* (Psalm 31:14).

> *"I will say of the LORD, 'He is my refuge and my fortress, my God, in whom I trust.'"* (Psalm 91:2).

You have to trust the Lord for who He is, that He is Your God, and the God of all creation. If you read all of Psalm 31 and 91 you'll come to understand David's trust in the Lord. Man, we too have got to trust Him like that if we're to complete this *"race of hope"* in flying colors. I insist that you read all of Psalms 31 and 91 meditatively and it will be a blessing to your soul. Are you going through trials? The safety jacket in this sea of trials and suffering is trust in God. It is what will keep your head lifted above the troubled waters. You have to trust Him for guidance and leadership daily, for protection against a million foes, for provision in the land of famine and thirst. You have to trust Him for healing and for deliverance every time, every day.

A single moment of doubt or distrust is like an hour *"off-guard"* for a soldier in a frontline battle and that off-guard hour is taken advantage of by the adversary. Your faith built for the long past may come crumbling like a tree cut from the roots and even if it doesn't crumble, it will be such that if *"even a fox climbed on it he would break down"* the shaken wall of faith.

Trusting in His Love

> *"But I trust in your unfailing love; my heart rejoices in your salvation"* (Psalm 13:5).

If you fail to trust the Lord because He is God, you can at least trust in His unfailing love, which He has shown you in diverse ways since your birth, and especially since your new birth. Every new day, God opens the infinite store of His unfailing love and lavishes it on His children and those who expect and long for His love shall benefit the most. For does not God show His love and at times we see it not? Can you list the ways in which God has shown you His love? Then since God is unchanging, continue to trust in His love and He shall unfold it to you in new ways that will go far beyond your comprehension. That's our God; He is a God of surprises and will continue to surprise you with impromptu gifts of His love as you trust in Him.

Trusting in His Word

> *"May your unfailing love come to me, O LORD, your salvation according to your promise; then I will answer the one who taunts me, for I trust in your word"* (Psalm 119:41-42).

There're folks who would taunt you about your faith, lifestyle, and the path you have chosen. Worse still there are those who will laugh at your failures and weaknesses. Only when you trust in God's word will you have the courage to press on and to answer those who taunt you. Remember people laughed at David and asked *"where is your God?"* He drew His reply from God's word. Man you have to believe God's word and everything in it if you're to stand the spite and mockery that comes from the world.

So we see that there're three places where your trust has to lie
1. In God Himself
2. In His unfailing love
3. In His faithful word

Now let's together look at some benefits which come as a result of trust. First of all let's look at why we trust and the implications of trust.

The Command to Trust

> *"Do not let your hearts be troubled. Trust in God; trust also in me"* (John 14:1).

For the child of God, trust is not an option but an obligation. Our blessed Lord gave us the command to trust and even if for this reason only, it suffices that you put your trust in Him. Lack of trust is therefore a manifestation of disobedience of this command given at such a critical moment of His dealings with His disciples. It is part of His last teachings given in His earthly ministry and so we trust because He has asked us to.

Notice that the command is placed just after He pointed out that Peter was going to deny Him and that all the others were going to run helter-skelter. He was saying *"in-spite of your failures, in-spite of the betrayal, do not despair, trust in the Father. You'll disappoint Me many times but do not trust in your might or your resolve or in any other virtue, but trust in the Father and in Me."*

The Implications of Trust

> *"Trust in the LORD with all your heart and lean not on your own understanding; in all your ways acknowledge him, and he will make your paths straight"* (Proverbs 3:5,6).

The implications of trust are very evident from the verses above;

- leaning not on your understanding
- acknowledging Him in all your ways

You know in this Christian race, many things will happen to us beyond our own understanding or ways of viewing things. There're many things you'll have to leave in the hand of God, for as you try to understand them you'll become increasingly confused and may even be led astray. There are moments you will just have to say Lord, I don't understand this but I accept it, for it comes from You. In whatever you do, wherever you are, you have to acknowledge Him, His power, love, goodness and faithfulness. To acknowledge, in this case, means to accept that God has all authority over you, no matter what He allows to come your way. He owes you nothing, yet you owe Him everything, including your comfort and very life which always seem threatened when trials come your way.

Trust implies that you know you are not your own, that you were bought with a price which nothing can measure, a price without an equivalent value in all creation. Trust implies saying *"Lord I am yours deal with me as you see best"*.

For What And When To Trust

"In all your ways" – in all you do, say, and think. There are no exceptions to the rule of trust. You must trust Him in all things, small or great, personal or general. You'll have to trust in Him at all times, when you succeed and when you fail, when you're weak and when you're strong, when you feel like and when you don't feel like, when you're afraid and when you're bold, when things are fine and when things are bad.

> *"Trust in him at all times, O people; pour out your hearts to him, for God is our refuge"* (Psalm 62:8).

> *"When I am afraid, I will trust in you. In God, whose word I praise, in God I trust; I will not be afraid. What can mortal man do to me?"* (Psalm 56:3-4)

Your sphere of trust has no bounds in time or in space.

The Benefits of Trust

First, trust gives you a sense of God's love.
> *"Many are the woes of the wicked, but the LORD's unfailing love surrounds the man who trusts in him"* (Psalm 32:10).

As you trust the Lord, you'll have a deep feeling of being surrounded by the immense personal love of God. This *"feeling"* of His love will envelop your soul and flood your heart. Even in the darkest night and most painful suffering you'll do nothing but thank Him for His love that is *"so deep that you can't get under it, so high that you can't get over it, so wide that you can't get out of it"*. It is when you trust that you have a true glimpse of His endless love.

Second, trust drives away fear.
He who trusts is not afraid of what man may do or of circumstances (see Psalm 56:4). My heart goes out to that song entitled *"My heart will trust"* by Mark Stevens in the Hillsong album *"shout to the Lord 2000"*. It is modeled from Psalm 23.

"Though I walk through valleys low I fear no evil; by the waters, still my soul, my heart will trust in You". The first stanza of that song says

"I'll walk closer now on the higher way, through the darkest night will you hold my hand, Jesus guide my way; O you mourn with me and you dance with me". That is what trust does, it drives away fear from the one who possesses it.

Third, trust does not only drive away fear, but it does bring confidence to the soul. Instead of being filled with fear, the one who trust is filled with courage and confidence.

> *"See, I lay in Zion a stone that causes men to stumble and a rock that makes them fall, and the one who trusts in him will never be put to shame"* (Romans 9:33).

The one who trusts is confident that tomorrow comes with a bounty of good things. He who trusts stands firm when all others fall, he takes his steps while all others are standing still. He is confident in all he does, yet his confidence is in the Lord his God.

Fourth, God cares for those who trust in Him.
> *"The LORD is good, a refuge in times of trouble. He cares for those who trust in him"* (Nahum 1:7).

As you maintain your peace and do not worry about the things that come your way, as you trust in Him, He'll take care of your every need. As you trust in Him and occupy yourself with the affairs of the Kingdom, He'll make sure you have the other things you need.

> *"But seek first his kingdom and his righteousness, and all these things will be given to you as well"* (Matthews 6:33).

Fifth, the strength of the Christian lies in trust.
The way is narrow and rugged. There'll be times when the climb seems so steep and every ounce of strength seems exhausted. In such times, strength comes from no other place but trust.

> *"In repentance and rest is your salvation, in quietness and trust is your strength…"* (Isaiah 50:15b).

Do you see that? You strength lies in holding your peace, maintaining a quiet spirit and trusting. Some people give up because they don't trust God to hold their hand and lead them on to the end hence they find no strength and therefore no reason to continue. But those who trust have strength in an infinite reservoir to tap from.

The sixth benefit of trust is that trust brings joy, peace and hope.
> *"May the God of hope fill you with all joy and peace as you trust in him, so that you may overflow with hope by the power of the Holy Spirit"* (Romans 15:13*).*

As you trust in God, He fills you with joy and peace. This means that when there's cause for gloom you'll be joyful, and when there's cause for worry and anxiety you'll portray a deep sense of inner peace. Thus, in this world of gloom and worry you'll live in your Island of joy and peace. These joy and peace will cause you to overflow with hope for a better and brighter day, hope for prosperity and blessing and this hope will flow out to others and contaminate them positively.

All these benefits of trust and others not mentioned here will make you to look like Mount Zion.

> *"Those who trust in the LORD are like Mount Zion, which cannot be shaken but endures forever"* (Psalm 125:1).

In other words, trust makes you stable, unshaken and persistent in all you do. Mount Zion is God's own holy mountain, a mount of blessing and interest. When Jesus comes He'll first appear on Zion. The Bible says if you trust in the Lord, you'll be like Mount Zion. May we all learn to trust our God and Father!

Chapter 17

More than just a Child

If we regard it form the world's view point, the highest point of one's relationship with God is that of child – Father. Any other thing comes below that. But kingdom-wise, there's a different way of viewing things, a different way of attributing values and standards which is quite contrary to the world. Remember we talked of two kingdoms. In the kingdom, our relationship with God as a Father is the most basic of all relationships with Him, for every other relationship must be built on this one. At conversion, we become children of God and as we grow in knowledge and intimacy we can become servants, and then grow to be friends of God. After becoming a friend, you can then become a slave of God.

Each higher level still depends on the lower ones. That is, although a child may not be a servant, every servant is a child and every slave means that person is also a child, a servant, and a friend of God. It is like moving from a child to a father, grandfather, then to a great grandfather. A great grandfather may still have his own father alive who calls him son. Do you understand that? I've heard people light-heartedly said they were friends to Jesus without understanding what it implies to be a friend of God. In this chapter we shall see some of the things which make us more than children of God.

The Child as a Servant

The first step of progress in the relationship between a Christian and God is that of growing into servanthood; the child growing into knowledge of God and the Lord Jesus as Master and we as the servant. We see in the world today, millions of people trying to become servants of God without the basic foundation of being children of God. God has no hired servants; everyone who serves Him must be one who bears His *"gene in Him"*, through the new birth in Christ Jesus. Without this basic, it is a total waste of time, energy and other resources.

God is not primarily interested in your service; He wants to make you, first of all His child. He wants to give you that privilege of being the child of the King of kings and Lord of lords, so that from the position of a child, you can understand His needs and longings and after having learnt obedience as a child, you can heartily obey Him as Master.

You see as Christians, we are called to follow Christ's example, walking in His footsteps in all we do. The Son of God and God the Son is referred to as the servant of the Lord (Isaiah 52 & 53). Before He became the servant of the Lord, He was first of all, God's One and only Son, from before the foundation of the world.

> *"Your attitude should be the same as that of Christ Jesus: Who, being in very nature God, did not consider equality with God something to be grasped, but made himself nothing, taking the very nature of a servant, being made in human likeness"* (Philemon 2:5-7).

The question might be asked as to how Christ served God; well throughout scripture service to God can be categorized into two main groups:

1. Serving God by serving the purposes of His kingdom
2. Serving God by serving fellow servants of God.

Serving God in Kingdom Purposes

As children, God has not called us to be spectators or onlookers to the things that are happening in His Kingdom. He has called us into active service, that we may speak things into existence and take part in building His Kingdom. It is but clear that service in God's kingdom is not limited. There're a thousand ways in which God can be served with respect to kingdom purposes, for *"There are different kinds of service but the same Lord"* (1 Corinthians 12:5). We're not all called to serve in the same way or in the same sphere but the end result is that we're serving God, in conformity to His Nature and methods as clearly revealed in the scriptures. A careful reading of 1 Corinthians 12:27-30, Ephesians 4:11-12, Romans 12:6-8, will give an extensive list of ministries through which we can serve in advancing the kingdom of God and having His will *"done on earth as it is in heaven"*.

You and I are just privileged, that we can be an active part in the building of an eternal Kingdom; we do not deserve to serve the King of the universe even in the remotest way, but thanks to His grace which made us children so we can become servants.

> *"So you also, when you have done everything you were told to do, should say, `We are unworthy servants; we have only done our duty"* (Luke 17:10).

It is nothing but a privilege to serve; we are nothing but *"unworthy servants"*. We do not serve to earn His love, or anything, though certainly there're rewards for services. However, this is not our aim, or at least it shouldn't be our aim. We serve because we've been given an opportunity to and because we owe Him our service, it is a duty we have to do.

In preaching the gospel, Paul said he was under obligation. You and I are under obligation to serve according to our gifts and talents. If God had not endowed us with gifts and talents, we would have an excuse for doing nothing in ensuring the advancement of His purposes here on earth, but there's so much He's invested in us and it is an obligation that we put it to use.

Whatever your gift or ministry, there's the basic responsibility of preaching the gospel to those around, whom we meet in the course of our daily activities. I find myself really wanting in this area of witnessing daily to sinners. We may not all have the responsibility of *"full-time evangelists"* but we all have to witness; we may not all have the responsibility of *"full-time intercessors"* but we're called to *"pray without ceasing"*; we're not all called to be *"full-time exhorters"* but we're all called to exhort and encourage one another. There're things which everybody can do and must do, only not to the same degree. It is of these which we'll be required to give an account on the Day of Judgment, for in the parable of the talents (Matthew 25) each one gave account according to the talents he was given.

Serving Servants

The most extensive way through which one may serve the Lord is by serving the saints – servants of God. You see, our human nature will always want to serve someone who's far elevated than one's own position. And God in His wisdom has decided that you and I serve one another, others who are themselves servants like you are. If it were just *"serving the Lord"*, many of us will quickly and happily accept to *"serve the Lord"*, after all He's God almighty, Maker of heaven and earth, King of kings and Lord of lords. Who wouldn't want to serve the King of the universe? God has made it clear, that those who'll serve Him, will serve His servants more, by praying, encouraging, helping, running errands etc. for them. It is this service rendered to man, which is a measure of greatness in the kingdom of God.

> *"Not so with you. Instead, whoever wants to become great among you must be your servant"* (Matthew 20:26).

Do you want to be great in the kingdom? Then serve the saints: not just those who seem to occupy *"high position in the church"*, not just those *"first class"* saints but those who may be considered *"the scum of the church"*, who have nothing to boast of as far as worldly possessions are concerned, those rejected by the community as a result of their profession of Christ, those who like their Master, *"have nothing in them which can attract the attention of men"*, no beauty, no majesty, just nothing in their appearance that they should be desired. Those who like their Master are despised and rejected even in the household of God – what sadness to say this, that some even in His house are rejected and despised, just because they can't measure up to the worldly standards which are creeping deep into the church, where people's influence no longer result from their Christlikeness but from how much money they have and of what social class they come from – those who like their Master are yet *"familiar with sufferings"* and know unceasing sorrow and anguish because of their faith.

These are the ones God is calling you and me to serve and by this we shall measure up to greatness in His kingdom. The condition of the Church today is that of division and strife leading to the creation of *"break away republics"*. There're *"Vaticans"* in the Roman Empire, all because we cannot heed to the counsel of becoming servants.

Are we responsible enough?

> *"Who then is the faithful and wise servant, whom the master has put in charge of the servants in his household to give them their food at the proper time? It will be good for that servant whose master finds him doing so when he returns. I tell you the truth, he will put him in charge of all his possessions. But suppose that servant is wicked and says to himself, `My master is staying away a long time,' and he then begins to beat his fellow servants and to eat and drink with drunkards. The master of that servant will come on a day when he does not expect him and at an hour he is not aware of. He will cut him to pieces and assign him a place with the hypocrites, where there will be weeping and gnashing of teeth"* (Matthew 24:45-51).

If Christ should return today won't He find us beating our fellow servants, dragging them in the mud? Won't He find us refusing to give them food at the proper time? Won't He find so many wounds inflicted on one another instead of the healing we were supposed to bring? I fear that unless there's an awakening in the Church of Christ today many a saint will be assigned *"a place with the hypocrites"* when our Master returns, for surely our attitude toward one another shows we are saying our *"Master is staying away a long time"*.

Permit me ask you some very personal questions:

What was your attitude towards that person you saw in need last time? What is your attitude towards that needy brother or sister by you? Do you prefer to give *"offering to church"* so your name be on the church's register as a faithful giver or meet the needs of a suffering servant which only you, the beneficiary and God will know about? Such things will deprive many saints from the honor they receive in their churches as a result of their *"show-off giving"*.

My brother, if you cannot meet the needs of someone by you, do not give to God, at least not the offering, for your money may end up only in the church's register with no records in heaven. Remember the rich young man in Mark 10 and the recommendation our Lord gave him? May we quote it here:

> *"Jesus looked at him and loved him. "One thing you lack," he said. "Go, sell everything you have and give to the poor, and you will have treasure in heaven. Then come, follow me"* (Mark 10:21).

Like him, many keep the commandments, without fault, they pay tithes regularly, pray regularly, read the scriptures regularly but lack one thing: *"to give to the poor"*. My heart goes out to *"operation blessings"* at CBN ministry, each time I watch them meet the needs of the poor in distant lands, what practice of Christianity indeed! If like Cornelius (Act 10), our *"prayers and gifts to the poor"* will go *"up as a memorial offering before God"* much will be accomplished as in the early church. May it be said of you that you *"give generously to those in need"*.

As individuals and as a church may we rise to meeting the needs of others, so that if Paul were with us he may say *"there is no need for me to write to you about this service to the saints"* (2 Corinthians 9:1), for after all *"This service that you perform is not only supplying the needs of God's people but is also overflowing in many expressions of thanks to God. Because of the service by which you have proved yourselves, men will praise God for the obedience that accompanies your confession of the gospel of Christ, and for your generosity in sharing with them and with everyone else"* (2 Corinthians 9:12-13).

How to Serve

There're rules which govern Christian service, be it in the advancement of the kingdom or in serving the saints. God has not left us to serve the way each one seems best, for that will bring a hell of chaos in whatever we consider service. Surely you'll find nowhere in scripture where rules for service are outlined like the ten commandment in Exodus 20. However any keen reader of the pages of the Book will come across too many of these guidelines to Christian service.

1. **Whole Hearted Service**

    "Serve wholeheartedly, as if you were serving the Lord, not men" (Ephesians 6:7).

    "Whatever you do, work at it with all your heart, as working for the Lord, not for men" (Colossians 3:23).

In the Christian life, there's no place for half-heartedness, not even when it is man who benefits from our services. God wants our full devotion. This brings us reward. Nothing done half-heartedly for God or man earns any reward in the kingdom of God.

2. **Serve in His Name:**

    "And whatever you do, whether in word or deed, do it all in the name of the Lord Jesus, giving thanks to God the Father through him" (Colossians 3:17).

All we do must be done in His Name, on the basis of His love, His grace, His mercy, His compassion on us and on others. We do not go in our own name, but in the Name of He who loves all and gave His life to bring us into the fullness of His blessings and riches.

3. **Serve with Zeal:**

   "Never be lacking in zeal, but keep your spiritual fervor, serving the Lord" (Romans 12:11).

Man if you're serving, serve with great energy and enthusiasm, as though that's the only opportunity to have to serve. The Bible says:-

   " Cursed be he that doeth the work of the Lord deceitfully, and cursed be he that keepeth back his sword from blood" (Jeremiah 48:10).

You may be working and serving, but as long as zeal is lacking, as long as there's no fervor in it you're cursed and that service will be of no benefit to those who receive it or to the kingdom of God. At the end all will be wasted time and resources.

4. **Serve with His Strength**

   "If anyone serves, he should do it with the strength God provides, so that in all things God may be praised through Jesus Christ" (1Peter 4:11b).

What a guideline! No place to brag about, no place to puff up about what you've done or are doing. No place to think lowly on others, no place for self-generated energy or strength as long as you serve in the kingdom. Serve in the strength and with the strength of the Lord. The purpose of this is so that God be glorified in all things. If you try to do it with your own strength, man you'll be left in the middle of it all. The only sure source of strength to go through whatever you do is the strength God provides, for this has no limit. That's why Paul could say *"To this end I labor, struggling with all his energy which so powerfully works in me"* (Colossians 1:29).

5. **Serve with Kindness**

   "And the Lord's servant must not quarrel; instead, he must be kind to everyone, able to teach, not resentful" (2 Timothy 2:24).

To serve kindly means to serve generously with care, friendliness and gentleness. Do not serve quarreling or grumbling or with reluctance. Serve with joy, consider it a privilege to serve and do it lovingly with tact. One may serve in kindness, no matter who you are serving. So be a kind-hearted servant of servants.

CHAPTER 18

THE CHILD AS A FRIEND

If you visit a home, as a guest, say for 3 days, you'll be quick to tell which child is a friend to the father or mother. This child will feel more at home with the father and talk freely with him. This reminds me of our youngest sister Daphne, who is such a friend to our father. Whenever he's around, she's always around him, talking and chatting and at times making jokes. When at school, she writes often sharing her difficulties with her Dad. Well, I'm more of a friend to my mother. I feel freer and more at home with her. She knows my moods even better than my father, and I too know her moods.

It is a similar thing with our heavenly Father. As children, we may grow into friends of God, yet there is no short cut to this. Every child must first of all be a servant before growing into a friend of God. No one becomes a friend of God without having offered a whole hearted service to Him for a period of time. Faithfulness in very small matters earns anyone the privilege to be called a friend of God.

It took the disciples three and a half years of careful following and obedience to Jesus. It took the disciples three and a half years of serving and being with Him, of going through thick and thin, tough and soft, together. The persecution He faced, they faced. The insults He suffered, they suffered, not forgetting the lonely nights with Him, the endless preaching of the gospel, healing of the sick and delivering the oppressed. They had tasted and exercised the power and authority of God's kingdom. Finally they were the ones who had communed with Him, whom He had personally taught and rescued from storms. I am quite sure it was with deepest delight, joy and gratitude that the disciples, on that eve of His crucifixion received promotion to friends of Jesus.

> *"I no longer call you servants, because a servant does not know his master's business. Instead, I have called you friends, for everything that I learned from my Father I have made known to you"* (John 15:15).

From this verse, we can draw three conclusions

1. Friendship with Jesus is a promotion from servanthood
2. A servant does not know everything about his master
3. On the basis of friendship, Jesus teaches His friends all He learns from the Father.

Thus we see that there're things a friend will know which the servant will have no idea about. Is it not why the life of some Christians is full of revelation while others are void of it? A friend of Jesus would know His joys, His sorrows, His needs and longings. Let us look at the examples of Abraham and Moses as friends of God.

Abraham God's Friend

> *"And the scripture was fulfilled that says, "Abraham believed God, and it was credited to him as righteousness," and he was called God's friend"* (James 2:23).

Actually this verse, at least the first part of it is a quotation from Genesis 15:6. It will be of good to take a few minutes and read through Genesis 15. Why was Abraham (then Abram) called God's friend? Because he believed God, took Him for His word and stood on His promises. Those who will become friends of God must believe all He says, and take Him for His word even in the darkest of moments. This absolute trust in God is followed by a promise which no one else will believe. It is on the basis of this friendship that God could say, *"Shall I hide from Abraham what I am about to do? Abraham will surely become a great and powerful nation, and all nations on earth will be blessed through him. For I have chosen him, so that he will direct his children and his household after him to keep the way of the LORD by doing what is right and just, so that the LORD will bring about for Abraham what he has promised him"* (Genesis 18:17-19).

And this is true. He hides nothing from His friends, at least not things that shall be of help or that will let them know Him better. It is on the basis of this friendship that Abraham could approach God, pleading the case of Sodom and Gomorrah and imploring God's mercy. Friends of God have a distinctive ministry which others can never partake of; they can approach God on matters which others can never dare to.

There's another side of the coin: friends of God will pass through tests that others won't experience. Theirs will be the hottest of furnaces, the most severe trials like what Abraham underwent, and in it all, they shall emerge victorious, joyous and purified, for the hand of their Friend will hold them through and His voice shall be their comfort.

Moses, God's Friend

> *"When a prophet of the LORD is among you, I reveal myself to him in visions, I speak to him in dreams. But this is not true of my servant Moses; he is faithful in all my house. With him I speak face to face, clearly and not in riddles; he sees the form of the LORD. Why then were you not afraid to speak against my servant Moses?"* (Number 12:6-8)

Moses, in all Bible history is the only one who has enjoyed such fellowship with God as God Himself describes it. He wasn't just a prophet, but a servant who new such intimacy with God, one of whom God said *"he is faithful in all my house"*. He was one servant whom God outrightly intervened to protect from slander and spite by other servants who held very high positions in the congregation which was matching across the desert. This description gives such an exalted view of the God – Moses relationship, which goes beyond any ordinary Master–servant relationship. It was indeed an extraordinary relationship that the only description the writer of Hebrew could give it is that of friend with friend:

> *"The LORD would speak to Moses face to face, as a man speaks with his friend"* (Exodus 33:11a).

God spoke with Moses as man speaks with his friend. Can you write down some qualities of a conversation between two friends? That's the kind of conversation Moses had with God each time they met. It is but clear that Moses' commitment to God was so unique and wholehearted. From the day God got hold of him, he responded with a wholehearted and reckless commitment to God and His purposes and to the Israelites too. This gave Moses, a mandate to approach God whenever and wherever, for whatever purpose. God revealed to him His form, His character and purpose like to no other. Moses was not just a servant of God Most High but a friend too.

A Friend so Close

> *"A man of many companions may come to ruin, but there is a friend who sticks closer than a brother"* (Proverbs 18:24).

My brother, there's a greater sphere of our relationship with the Lord which is beyond the ordinary. It is to become a friend of God, a friend of Jesus. He's the most faithful friend you can ever find. He's never too busy to listen, to offer His help in times of need. He's always there to lead and to direct.

What a blessing to be a friend to Jesus. The problem is that most of us are still at the level of servants, when we serve faithfully and wholeheartedly, we shall receive our promotion to the level of friends. He is a friend who will share all your pains and joy; He'll dance with you and mourn with you. At the level of friendship, there's a total unity of purpose with His. His burdens become your burdens; His wishes become your command. In situations where a brother will run away, this Friend of yours will stick close.

Is it not so amazing that mortals will have the immortal King of the universe as a Friend? What elevation! What honor! What glory! The truth is that I find no illustration to this, no human relationship whatsoever can measure up to it in the remotest of ways. It is a relationship far beyond what words can express, beyond the comprehension of the most enlightened human mind. He's a Friend with no secret motive behind His friendship, no selfish interest. He has all to offer you and nothing to gain. The hymn writer could say:

> "I've found a friend, o such a friend,
> He loved me, ere I new Him,
> He drew me with the chords of love
> And thus He bond me to Him
> And round my heart still closely twine
> Those chords which not can server
> And I am His and He is mine, forever and forever".

This hymn could only flow out of intimacy with the Savior, out of a life which knew such identification with the Master in will and in interest. May we all grow to be His friend too, and then our lips shall be filled with love songs to this Friend so unique, so pure, so true and so close. May we long with earnestness to make progress in servant-hood, then in due time, we shall each receive our promotion to the level of friends of God.

A Friend to Trust

One thing which causes many a human friendship to crumble is lack of mutual trust, at least from one side of the relationship. Here and there, there's a cry of foul, of betrayal, of mistrust, of suspicion, many have gotten into relationships whole only to come out in pieces and broken heartedness. Many a man or a woman walks along the street with no sense of security, no trust in anyone, for one he or she thought was a trusted friend gave a deadly blow of betrayal, and now their eyes classify all humans as traitors. Usually in his or her world, there's no one to share her fears with, no hands into which she can cry her tears. Her past experience of friendship is just a nightmare and there is this built-in hatred for all who attempt to draw close. The gates into her world are shut and bolted, with the password which she alone and the all-knowing God know. All attempts to get into her world will only meet repulsion.

For some it is not a lack of trust but the fact that circumstance seem to separate them from whoever they have labored to build a trusted friendship with. The pain of death has separated others from the friend they so trusted and hence they find no need to build any new relationship. Well that's the picture of our earthly friendship! I should not be understood as having said, there're no successful human friendships, some have succeeded, others are succeeding and others still will succeed.

Are you looking for someone you can trust as a friend? Jesus is right there for you. One thing is sure, the Christian life will have a new meaning and will offer a new hope if you and I will become friends of our Savior and Lord. There'll be a new strength to face trials and to suffer for His sake; the wounds we may incur in our Christian life will be seen through different eyes. Why? It is because, *"wounds from a friend can be trusted"* (Proverbs 27:6).

I want to say that is not just a matter of viewing Jesus as a friend, not a wish nor an imagination but actually being a friend of His which brings along this sense of confidence and of hope. Once a friend of His, you shall see trials, sufferings and whatever may befall you, as acts of love coming from a trusted Friend. Failure and weakness will be accepted and used positively. There'll be a new sense of positivity in the Christian life. Where others see rejection and abandonment you'll see love and care, where other despair you'll have hope. He's a Friend so rich whom you'll trust for provision, a Friend so powerful whom you'll trust for protection, a Friend so wise, whom you'll trust for counseling, with arms into which you can run at any time and receive rest like a baby. May be one could ask:

> *"Did ever saint find this friend forsake him?*
> *No not one! No not one!"*

I am quite sure, one saint after living as a servant for such a long period was brought into the thrilling experience of knowing Christ Jesus as a friend. He never failed to express his discovery of this *"new world"* in a classic hymn sung all over, especially in times of need. What encouragement it brings; what inspiration. The day we too shall arrive or discover this new world of friendship, we shall each burst out with songs similar to this one, and surely day and night, they shall flow forth from our lips.

Chapter 19

THE CHILD AS A SLAVE

This level of relationship with our Savior is the highest of all. It is what I may term voluntary slavery. It is an overflow of friendship with the Lord. In Christian history, very few have attained this conscious laying down of all rights as a friend, a voluntary giving up of all benefits of this friendship. This is the highest level of response to grace and just few have attained it and yet it is the goal of still a few.

> *"Greater love has no one than this, that he lay down his life for his friends"* (John 15:13).

Such love for your friend will cause you to despise comfort, gain and pleasure, to despise and defile circumstances so your trusted friend's heart can be satisfied. This overflow of the love relationship caused some people to yearn to suffer for His sake. Let's look at a few of them:

> *"Here I am, Lord, send me; send me to ends of the earth; send me to the rough, the savage pagans of the wilderness; send me from all that is called comfort on earth, or earthly comfort: send me to death itself, if it be but in thy service and to promote thy kingdom"* David Brained.

> *"Yet more; oh, my God, more toil, more agony, more suffering for Thee"* Francis Xavier.

> *"If Jesus Christ be God and died for me, then no sacrifice can be too great for me to make for Him"* C.T. Studd.

Again may I remind you, that this is not forced labor, it is voluntary slavery which flows out from a heart united to God's, from a purpose tied to His, from a will surrendered to His, from the life of one who has laid all rights on the altar of the gospel of Christ Jesus. It is at this level of relationship that you and I may take the world for our God.

Paul knew this thrilling relation and gives us a tip of his experience.

> *"Rather, as servants of God we commend ourselves in every way: in great endurance; in troubles, hardships and distresses; in beatings, imprisonments and riots; in hard work, sleepless nights and hunger"* (2 Corinthians 6:4-5).

> *"I have worked much harder, been in prison more frequently, been flogged more severely, and been exposed to death again and again. Five times I received from the Jews the forty lashes minus one. Three times I was beaten with rods, once I was stoned, three times I was shipwrecked, I spent a night and a day in the open sea, I have been constantly on the move. I have been in danger from rivers, in danger from bandits, in danger from my own countrymen, in danger from Gentiles; in danger in the city, in danger in the country, in danger at sea; and in danger from false brothers. I have labored and toiled and have often gone without sleep; I have known hunger and thirst and have often gone without food; I have been cold and naked. Besides everything else, I face daily the pressure of my concern for all the churches"*
> (2 Corinthians 11:23b-28).

This is the life of one mastered by God, so one would say, they were slaves of God, for Peter said *"a man is a slave to whatever has mastered him"* (2 Peter 2:19b).

The Child as Co-Worker

Whether servants or friends or slaves of God, we all are His co-workers. In fact we are His workmanship, seeking to advance His Kingdom.

> *"For we are God's fellow workers; you are God's field, God's building."* (1 Corinthians 3:9a).

That's what we are; we work hand in glove with God, as partners. What elevation! We work with God, with Him we decide the course of the earth, and we all belong to the parliament that governs the earth. Blessed be the Lord, who chose you and me to become His fellow-workers.

You see! You are not just a child who knows nothing about his father's business, but your heavenly Father has made you a fellow-worker of His. Our goal is to see His kingdom come upon the earth, to establish the reign of our God and His Christ, to see His will done on every corner and in every life. That is our task – the building of an eternal kingdom and we do it together with God.

He chose you and me to partake in this glorious task. Through us, God is making His appeal of reconciliation to a world that has gone astray and lives in total rebellion and hostility towards the Lord and His purposes. As God's co-workers, He has not left us to ourselves but puts at our disposal Angels to render us ministry:

> *"Are not all angels ministering spirits sent to serve those who will inherit salvation?"* (Hebrews 1:14).

What honor, to be served by angels-celestial beings, why? Because we are God's workmanship. They are there to offer us protection, to help us in our time of need, to carry God's messages to us. They carry our requests to God and bring from Him responses. Many times, they go ahead of us to prepare the way. Truly, angels are there, always by us, watching how we carry out our daily responsibilities as co-workers, and taking reports to God. In the commonest term, angels act as body guards, and run our errands. You see the privilege of co-working with God?

If you and I as co-workers meet and decide or agree on anything, heaven puts its seal on it and it is validated, without any *"higher house of parliament"* going through it. We have ready access to our *"Boss"* whenever wherever we are. No need to book any appointment, no need to travel any distance, we have a *"Boss"* who's omnipresent and who makes no mistakes.

Furthermore, we aren't just ordinary co-workers. We are heaven's special envoys here on earth. *"We are therefore Christ's ambassadors"* (2 Corinthians 5:20). Here on earth, we carry with us heaven's seal and issue out passports to the *"Land of Glory"*. To us God has issued responsibility of reconciliation as it is written, *"all this is from God, who reconciled us to himself through Christ and gave us the ministry of reconciliation: that God was reconciling the world to himself in Christ, not counting men's sins against them. And he has committed to us the message of reconciliation"* (2 Corinthians 5:18,19b).

May I give you the definition of an ambassador: An ambassador is an official who lives in a foreign country as a senior representative of his or her own country. The world in ignorance may despise us, call us mean names and treat us with contempt. They may regard us as insane, as people without any future, frustrated and a bunch of fools. But one thing is sure, we know what we are: *"senior representatives"* of heaven here in this base foreign land, which is no equal to our Homeland. It can't even measure up to one-trillionth of it.

Take us out of this world and it suffers the setbacks of the absence of heaven's envoys. No special aid from heaven, no rescue missions, for who will be there to mediate? There's no analogy one can draw in this earth to explain the degree of our elevation. Ours is an office without retirement. We have no constrain as to how many visas to issue per year. We issue as many as we can.

Our homeland longs to meet the needs of the inhabitants of this foreign territory and to grant them a transfer of kingdoms and free naturalization, no complicated procedure. All they need to do is pledge allegiance to the King of our Homeland and abide to the ways of the Kingdom. We offer asylum to those seeking refuge, who are escaping terror and horror of a cruel head of their own kingdom. We offer health to those suffering from diseases inflicted by the rulers of their kingdom, we storm their jails to release their captives and oppressed, so they too can enjoy the freedom we have.

CHAPTER 20

THE CHILD IN THE FATHER'S ARMY

The day we pledge allegiance to the kingdom of God, we each become a soldier of the cross of Calvary. As imperialists, we have the duty to get everything to obey our commander in chief, the glorious Lord Jesus Christ.

Oh that battle cry that sounds
In hearts that are filled
With passion and vision
From the light of heaven

The mighty cry that thunders
A call to subdue and conquer
Everything that has breathe
For the glory of its Creator

A cry that spurs someone
From within the inner man
To be filled with zeal
And proclaim the Good News

The mighty cry to repentance
To crush and smitten
Every resistance on the way
Imposing the will of our God

Oh battle cry that rages
A cry of Calvary's victory
Possessing every land and nation
For the glory of the King of heaven
E.C. Nakeli 2000

That's the nature of our battle - taking captive every thought, philosophy and doctrine contrary to that of our Homeland and bringing every knee to bow in homage to our King and Savior. No child is exempted: whether servants or friends or slaves, all are on the battlefield and there's no retreat for no neutral ground is available. You belong to one of the armies, no neutrality. To us subjects of the kingdom the command is to *"Endure hardship with us like a good soldier of Christ Jesus"* (2 Timothy 2:3), as we all are cautioned to be alert and watching because *"No one serving as a soldier gets involved in civilian affairs – he wants to please his commanding officer"* (2 Titus 2:4).

Man as a soldier, you are to put away the unnecessary. Besides we're not called to a *"bread and tea battle"*. Ours is a difficult one, no playing about. Our goal is not first to fight but to please our commander in chief. All orders come from Him. We invade territories at His command. In this war, no civilian causalities are involved, for everyone is a soldier. The urgency and loudness of this cry sounds more in hearts filled with passion and vision from above. The words of this hymn explain it better.

Stand up, stand up for Jesus
Ye soldiers of the cross,
Lift high His royal banner
It must not suffer loss

The Magnitude of Our Enemy

You and I are engaged in no ordinary battle, our foes are without number. His strength is far beyond ours as the hymn writer gives a picture of it:

> *"For still our ancient foe*
> *Doth seek to work his woe*
> *His craft and power are great*
> *And armed with cruel hate –*
> *On earth is not his equal*
> (SS&S hymn 2, selected)

That's why you and I are called to stand in the strength of Jesus alone. Paul gives us a picture of our adversaries:

> *"For our struggle is not against flesh and blood, but against the rulers, against the authorities, against the powers of this dark world and against the spiritual forces of evil in the heavenly realms"* (Ephesians 6:12).

That's the nature of the adversary: his methods and techniques, the degree of his hatred, words may not describe. But we need not fret; God has not left us alone. He is right there in the battle with us and supplies us with weapons and techniques. We have an armor mighty to defend us against his attacks and we have a weapon to keep him on the run. In the Name of the Victor – Jesus Christ, we force him to retreat from territories once illegally occupied. Though he's been defeated he bluffs about and claims ownership of what is another's both by creation and by redemption.

The Soldiers Armor

Man, God has provided to you an amour mighty enough to resist and defend yourself from the continuous assaults on us by the enemy of our souls. Ours is the responsibility to put on the amour and learn how to walk about in it so in the day of danger we shall not need to have an emergency training session. Who then is prepared for the battle? He who has his complete armor on.

> *"Therefore put on the full armor of God, so that when the day of evil comes, you may be able to stand your ground, and after you have done everything, to stand. Stand firm then, with the belt of truth buckled around your waist, with the breastplate of righteousness in place, and with your feet fitted with the readiness that comes from the gospel of peace. In addition to all this, take up the shield of faith, with which you can extinguish all the flaming arrows of the evil one. Take the helmet of salvation and the sword of the Spirit, which is the word of God. And pray in the Spirit on all occasions with all kinds of prayers and requests. With this in mind, be alert and always keep on praying for all the saints"* (Ephesians 6:13-18).

From this passage, we readily bring out the following objects of defense.

1. **The Belt of Truth**

    He who is prepared for battle is one who has a deep and clear knowledge of the truth, one with a profound and radical commitment to speaking and living truth. Without this, there's a handicap for that soldier and one day, he shall be arrested for trafficking of illegal goods of lies in the kingdom of truth and shall be found wanting. A soldier who is found wanting by his own army, has no place in the battle. The deep knowledge of Bible truth gets the soldier to know the grounds on which the battle is fought, why we're fighting, the promises which we carry as soldiers. Without this knowledge, you shall be deceived.

2. **The Breastplate of Righteousness:**

    This signifies a life which always does what is right. It talks of total obedience to God and to the Commander in Chief. There's nothing that makes us vulnerable to defeat and failure like disobedience. In this battle, you'll have to take and keep orders even when they sound foolish. There is no place for arguments or quarreling with the commander in chief, or for rebellion towards God. Thus any rebellion will mean identifying yourself with the enemy and you'll find yourself in the military tribunal to answer for treason.

3. **Feet Ready to Proclaim the Gospel of Peace:**

This talks of earnestness in service, being ever ready to serve the King with zeal. Remember the five guidelines to service.

4. **The Shield of Faith:**

This is an unwavering believe that God will do what He has promised. Standing on His word in spite of contrary evidences. It is the strong yet simple trust and hope in Christ; His person, works and truth. It is believing who God is as revealed in His word. This brings in "the child's responsibility to trust" maybe you take a look at it once more. You know the flaming arrows of the evil one are put out by the shield of faith. The breastplate is there to deal only with the few which may be swift to come through.

5. **The Helmet of Salvation:**

You know, one of the ways through which the adversary attacks is by putting doubts in your heart about your stand with God. The one ready for such a battle must have a full assurance of his salvation and relation to God. Without this, you have no mandate to launch any attack from this side of the battle line. This side belongs to those who are sure of having being saved, washed and sanctified by the blood of the Lamb of God. Doubters of this fact are still vulnerable to a greater defeat, for they are "illegal immigrants" in the army. If this is your case, man you had better correct things.

These make up the armor of defense. Any of it lacking will mean vulnerability to defeat.

The Magnitude of Our Weapons

> "The weapons we fight with are not the weapons of the world. On the contrary, they have divine power to demolish strongholds. We demolish arguments and every pretension that sets itself up against the knowledge of God, and we take captive every thought to make it obedient to Christ. And we

> *will be ready to punish every act of disobedience, once your obedience is complete" (2 Corinthians 10:4-6).*

That's the magnitude of our weapons; weapons with divine power – God's own power. What are they capable of doing? They are capable of demolishing strongholds – i.e. pulling and knocking them down easily and completely. That's what our weapons are capable of doing. Now having seen the magnitude of our weapons, what then are the weapons:

1. The word of God
2. prayer

The Word of God – The Sword of the Spirit.

> *"For the word of God is living and active. Sharper than any double-edged sword, it penetrates even to dividing soul and spirit, joints and marrow; it judges the thoughts and attitudes of the heart"* (Hebrews 4:12).

Do you remember the confrontation in the wilderness between the King of glory and the traitor prince? How was it won? By the proclamation of the word of God, our Lord just quoted the scriptures and victory came. In this warfare, there're moments when you'll just have to speak out the word in situations and gain your victory. This calls for a careful and diligent study and mastery of the word.

As you store the Word in your heart, in times of emergency the Spirit will help you draw strength from this *"oil reserve"* to keep your lamp burning. Without this reserve, your lamp will go out as a result of a shortage in time of emergency and what danger to walk in the dark.

"It penetrates even to dividing soul and spirit" The word gives one a distinction between the carnal and the spiritual; that which originates from the outside and from the inside. The word, when mastered, shall help you distinguish between confidence in the flesh and confidence in the Lord. Remember everything which originates from the flesh is illegal in this warfare no matter how sophisticated it may appear. Success in using the weapon of prayer depends on

one's mastery of the word, for all true and effective praying must be founded on God's Word.

The Weapon of Prayer:

Below are some facts about prayer, drawn from S.D. Gordon's *"Quiet talks on prayer"*

- Prayer is projecting one's spirit personally
- Prayer is using your spirit to influence spirit beings surrounding a particular situation or person.
- Prayer is insisting upon Jesus' victory and the retreat of the enemy on each particular spot, and heart and problem concerned.
- Prayer must be persistent.
- The praying person is the one foe among men whom Satan cannot withstand; he is projecting an irresistible spirit force into the spirit realm.
- Prayer is man giving God a footing on the contested territory of this earth.
- The man wholly given over to God gives Him a new sub-headquarters on the battle field from which to work out.
- The greatest outlet of spiritual power is prayer.

For more on prayer, see the prayer power series by Professor Z.T. Fomum. At the moment, there are books one to ten and they contain an enormous wealth of teaching on prayer.

Having seen the weapons we have and their magnitude what then are the targets of the soldier of the cross?

Our Targets

Our targets as soldiers are the strongholds of the enemy (see 2 Corinthians 10:4b). Remember he is our enemy, and our aim is to destroy his strongholds completely. You know Satan has his strongholds on which all his other works or arsenals hold. Paul, has not failed to give us his strongholds.

1. Arguments
2. Pretension
3. Evil thoughts
4. Disobedience

The truth is that every work of Satan, every sin can be linked to either an argument, a pretension, an evil thought, or disobedience. There is no need fighting his other works if the strongholds are still standing. I believe the church will make such a rapid progress in causing the enemy to retreat if we concentrate and direct our weapons to his strongholds. For once the strongholds fall, all else which depends on them will fall, never to rise again.

Consider the stronghold of arguments. Every philosophy, every false doctrine, every false religion is built on nothing but these arguments which set themselves up against the knowledge of Christ and of God. They include arguments that Christ is not the only way to God, that man is answerable to himself, that there is neither hell nor heaven. In our battle, this is what we are to launch against.

Take the stronghold of pretension. The greatest evil which hides in this stronghold is religion.

Religion is the devil's most subtle of strategies to keep people bound. If this stronghold is not dealt with, millions will continue to live in presumption, *"having a form of godliness but denying its power"* (2Timothy 3:5a). Other sins like hypocrisy, backbiting and gossip find their shelter too under the stronghold of pretension. And unless pretension is dealt with, no matter how much weapon is fired on those sins, they will still rise up some time later, for new strength or reinforcement shall come from their stronghold.

Take the stronghold of evil thoughts. This is the birthplace and power source of many a sin. It is said that the thoughts of a man makes the man. Every sin can well be traced to an evil thought, which gives birth to evil desires which lead to sin. To wage war against symptoms without having taken care of the source is nothing but folly. By demolishing this stronghold of evil thoughts, many other sins like malice, hatred, bitterness, un-forgiveness, sexual immorality, lies telling will be dealt with.

Making the Difference in the Battle

Like in the days of the Judges, the church kind of finds herself impotent before the enemy. The war against conformity to worldly standards and religion seems to be on a loss, and the effect is that increasingly, some sins are being tolerated in some Christian circles. I can't express in words the shock with which I ended one day, after hearing the response to a question asked a telvangelist by a teenage girl. It was on premarital kissing, and all the preacher could say is that *"provided it will lead to marriage it isn't wrong"*. What a lie from the enemy. I fear for the many souls that will be wrecked as a result of heeding that response. I do not see how intimate kissing before marriage won't lead to sexual thoughts and desire and lust.

All of us are aware of the scandal about the appointment of a gay bishop in the U.S Episcopal Church. I wonder why such a man could be allowed in the church of the First Born, let alone in the spiritual office. This only shows how rotten, many a denomination is. What apostasy! What derailment!

Well I believe this was just a symptom of a longtime disease that had been eating deep into that "church" without being taken care of. As earlier mentioned, the church seems to be losing ground in several dimensions, in many cases, it stems from the fact that many a leader has forfeited all rights to the Spirit's anointing, power and authority. Yet there're many who're disturbed by this. They are waiting for one who will rise across the world to lead a militant battle against the enemy infiltration.

Thank God for those who are already there and are *"leading"* this battle to victory. They are current day *"God's generals"* but there's need for more, if the next generation should by any means be handed down the teaching on holiness and purity and unconditional obedience to God. God is looking for volunteers, who will be willing to *"lead"* this battle.

> *"When the princes in Israel take the lead, when the people willingly offer themselves-- praise the LORD! ... My heart is with Israel's princes, with the willing volunteers among the people. Praise the LORD!"* (Judges 5:2 and 9)

Though at times God may appoint specific people for specific services, most of His choices are based on voluntary offers of lives to Him. His constant appeal is *"whom shall I send? And who will go for us?"* And surly He waits for who shall reply "Here am I, send me". His response then shall be *"Go and tell this people"* – the people of your generation, the ones whom His Son died for. (See Isaiah 6:8 - 9).

The truth is that God's heart is with the willing volunteers among the saints. He will not withhold His approval, His favor and resources, from those who willingly volunteer to go to the frontline (Read I Samuel 17), provided they do so in His Name alone. My brother, my sister, offer yourself to Him and you shall be a vessel in His hand, to bring to fulfillment His plans and purposes, and He shall be your delight, your portion, your inheritance. The princes of the kingdom are the willing volunteers among the saints. He longs for your willingness to be His herald, and would withhold nothing back to approve a course which brings Him all the glory. So you can make a difference if you heed to the call for *"front liners"*.

CHAPTER 21

THE CHILD AS LIGHT

"You are the light of the world" (Matthew 5:14a).
"In the same way, let your light shine before men, that they may see your good deeds and praise your Father in heaven" (Matthew 5:16).

Take us out of the world and everything goes sour and dark and void. As a believer, you're light to the world; it is your responsibility to light the world around you and beyond. You know the coming of Christ Jesus into one's life is like the lighting of the lamp of one's soul. This lamp when lit cannot be hidden but illumines the whole person from the spirit within, to the body outside. The soul is like the lampstand which carries and supports the lamp. The illumination of one's being is expressed primarily through the soul, which is the mind, will and emotions of the person.

The spirit of a man is the channel through which fuel flows to keep this lamp burning. In most cases, when the heart is used in scripture, it talks of the innermost being of man-his spirit. When our Lord Jesus said *"Blessed are the pure in heart for they shall see God"*, He meant that, *"Blessed are the pure in spirit for they shall see God"*. This purity in spirit ensures a smooth flow of oil from God's infinite reservoir – the indwelling Holy Spirit, to the soul of man to keep the lamp burning. Once the heart is impure, the channel becomes blocked and there's no flow of oil hence the lamp fades out and finally goes off.

The first thing anyone would come in contact with is your soul; your will, mind and emotions. From these, one can tell whether a soul is illumined or not and whether it has run out of oil or keeps a constant supply. Once the soul is illumined, the whole man is illumined and becomes a *"light of the world"*. Your presence anywhere should bring light to the darkness around, as people will see your life, expressed in doing what is good and right and pure. So go light your world.

Paul tells us, how you light your world, he says to *"Do everything without complaining or arguing, so that you may become blameless and pure, children of God without fault in a crooked and depraved generation, in which you shine like stars in the universe"* (Philippians 2:14-15).

Yeah! In this world of crooks and perverts, we are called to be blameless, pure and faultless and thus shine like stars. Thus we're not ordinary common light, we are star lights, as long as we live blameless, pure and faultless lives. You see just as it is difficult to see a star on a foggy or cloudy day, so it will be if you allow any sin in your life. It shall act as a fog and prevent your light from being seen. The church is *"a city on a hill"* visible to all around, and the life of the inhabitants of that city, you and I, is expressed to all who pass by. If we really light our world, those out of that city will long to become part of it.

A New Purpose For Living

I received in the course of writing this book, a news which kept me broken for some time, the news of the death of the second Vice President of the Ministry in which I fellowship (CMFI). This news sent waves of panic and bewilderment throughout the world, among members of our ministry. This warrior of God died in a ghastly motor accident, at the prime of his life, a 45 year-old man, one who was in charge of Cameroon Conquest for Jesus, the personal interpreter of Professor Fomum. His death brought untold pain and agony to the entire ministry, but one thing was sure, he had lived for God, he had a right purpose for living, totally caught up with his God and his work.

Few people nowadays measure up to the level of his consecration to God. He had lived a simple life, yet lived to the full for his God. From his death, there's one thing I learnt: no one has any guarantee for tomorrow as James said, *"Why, you do not even know what will happen tomorrow. What is your life? You are a mist that appears for a little while and then vanishes"* (James 4:14). This short time one has to live, one must make the greatest impact for God. It is in this light that we'll close this book, a call to respond to the new purpose of living.

> *"And he died for all, that those who live should no longer live for themselves but for him who died for them and was raised again"* (2 Corinthians 5:15).

You and I were saved, not to live for ourselves, not to serve our own interest, but to live for Him who gave His all so we could be set free from bondage to sin and slavery to Satan. The call is for you and me to abandon our own plans and embrace the plan of our Father. Let us invest our lives for our God; after all we belong to another.

> *"So, my brothers, you also died to the law through the body of Christ, that you might belong to another, to him who was raised from the dead, in order that we might bear fruit to God"* (Romans 7:4).

That is our only guarantee, a life lived totally and purposely for God, so we can truly identify with Paul in saying, *"For none of us lives to himself alone and none of us dies to himself alone. If we live, we live to the Lord; and if we die, we die to the Lord. So, whether we live or die, we belong to the Lord"* (Romans 14:7-8).

Conclusion

I wrote this book almost 13 years ago from the depth of my heart. It is a challenge to all of us to live our lives to the fullest for Christ and His Kingdom. If you have been blessed by this book and would like to share with us please write to:

    E. C. Nakeli,
    CMFI Maryland
    40 S Church st
    Westminster, MD 21157

Other publications from the publisher

Other publications from the publisher

Other publications from the publisher

Other publications from the publisher

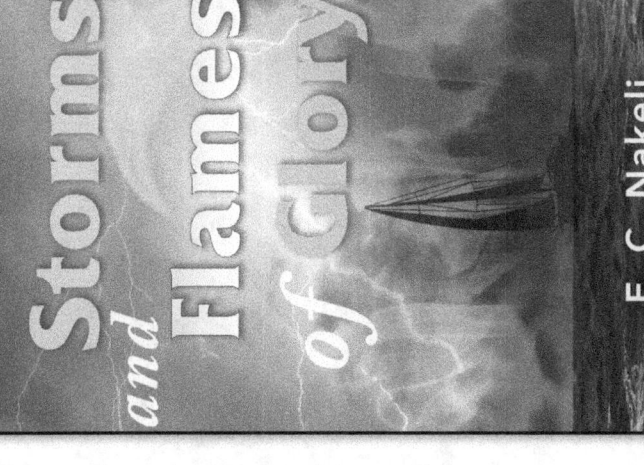

www.ingramcontent.com/pod-product-compliance
Lightning Source LLC
Chambersburg PA
CBHW071621080526
44588CB00010B/1209